Students in Urban Settings:
Achieving the Baccalaureate Degree

by Richard C. Richardson, Jr., and Louis W. Bender

ASHE-ERIC Higher Education Report No. 6, 1985

Prepared by

 ® *Clearinghouse on Higher Education*
The George Washington University

Published by

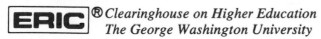

Association for the Study of Higher Education

Jonathan D. Fife,
Series Editor

Cite as
Richardson, Richard C., Jr., and Bender, Louis W. *Students in Urban Settings: Achieving the Baccalaureate Degree*. ASHE-ERIC Higher Education Report No. 6. Washington, D.C.: Association for the Study of Higher Education, 1985.

The ERIC Clearinghouse on Higher Education invites individuals to submit proposals for writing monographs for the Higher Education Report series. Proposals must include:
1. A detailed manuscript proposal of not more than five pages.
2. A 75-word summary to be used by several review committees for the initial screening and rating of each proposal.
3. A vita.
4. A writing sample.

Library of Congress Catalog Card Number 85-073509
ISSN 0884-0040
ISBN 0-913317-25-X

ERIC® **Clearinghouse on Higher Education**
The George Washington University
One Dupont Circle, Suite 630
Washington, D.C. 20036

ASHE **Association for the Study of Higher Education**
One Dupont Circle, Suite 630
Washington, D.C. 20036

This publication was partially prepared with funding from the National Institute of Education, U.S. Department of Education under contract no. 400-82-0011. The opinions expressed in this report do not necessarily reflect the positions or policies of NIE or the Department.

EXECUTIVE SUMMARY

The public policy undergirding American higher education is directed toward the ideal of equality and equity of educational opportunity. An array of institutions having significantly different missions and program emphases has been established in response to that public policy. An implicit assumption is that students who begin in an open access institution will, if successful, be able to move to other institutions providing different and more advanced opportunities. Many studies of efforts to achieve articulation between quite different institutions have been carried out over the years, but inadequate attention has been given to urban areas where the greatest challenge to the goal of equality of opportunity exists. Simply stated, more poor people, more minorities, and more immigrants live in cities where the college-age population is still less than half as likely to enroll in college as their suburban counterparts.

How Is America's Population Changing?
The demographic profile of American children now entering public schools makes it clear the problems for urban colleges and universities will grow in magnitude in the years ahead. The ethnic composition of Americans has shifted, caused by a drop in the birth rate among whites over the last two decades while birth rates among minorities remained the same or increased (Feistritzer 1985). The white percentage of total population dropped from 87.4 percent in 1970 to 83.2 percent in 1980. Blacks now represent 12 percent of the total population and will increase their percentage in the years ahead. The fastest growing minority, however, is persons of Hispanic origin. The trend is of special significance for the urban city, where 54.2 percent of all black children in this nation live and where the Hispanic minorities also are disproportionately located. The same areas are absorbing the bulk of foreign-born immigrants who are coming to America at an increased rate and among whom the degree of English proficiency can be a related educational disadvantage.

The poverty level in the United States grew from 11.1 percent in 1973 to 15.2 percent in 1983, with minority groups experiencing most of that increase. One-third of all children living in inner cities are poor, and over half of the poor are black. Even family composition is changing. One-parent households are increasing, and one-half of those children who do live with both parents are latchkey children because both parents are working.

A correlation exists between income and education achieved. Low-income students do not achieve as well, persist as long, or complete programs of study in the same proportion as students from middle- and upper-income groups, who typically have had the advantage of greater encouragement and support at home, better schools offering more academic preparation, and a cultural expectation of a collegiate education.

How Are Urban Colleges and Universities Responding?
Responsibility for the higher education needs of the inner city population has fallen primarily to the public urban universities and community colleges. Tied organically to their cities, both types of institution share the problems of the urban environment. Both must deal with such conditions as poverty among students, high attrition, failing school systems, and limited institutional funding. An examination of their working relationships reveals such similar institutional problems as confusing missions, overvaluing traditional ways at the expense of the local community's needs, undervaluing institutional cooperation, and failing to communicate (Cafferty and Spangenberg 1983).

Urban community colleges do confront enormous problems, and they are the only alternative for most of the students they serve. They have emphasized to a considerable degree establishing a supportive environment for minority students, and they have demonstrated a significant advantage in providing underprepared students the time and support to remedy academic deficiencies. The preponderance of evidence suggests students who complete two-year academic transfer programs at community colleges perform reasonably well after they transfer. Yet a critical view of colleges serving minorities in one city grows out of a recent study that found the inner city community colleges more inclined to emphasize remedial and vocational programs while offering only a semblance of transfer education (Orfield et al. 1984). Furthermore, the actual academic course offerings were found to be narrower and more limited in the city colleges than in their suburban counterparts. Course completion rates were low, student advising minimal, and part-time faculty predominant at the inner city campuses.

Urban universities have diverse missions, purposes, and emphases (Rudnick 1983; Smartt 1981). Their ambiguity of mission makes achieving a satisfactory definition difficult. Some quest to achieve the status of the traditional residential university, while others serve a regional clientele. They consistently emphasize the economic development of the urban area involved and commit themselves to professional and technical programs, as contrasted to undergraduate arts and sciences. They reflect their location by providing programs that serve the basic educational needs of place-bound and traditionally underrepresented clienteles but typically see these activities as detrimental to their image as research institutions. While urban community colleges and universities recognize the importance of the transfer student, the two institutions have not been linked in any way to make this process systematic and orderly. In several cities, they compete for the better-prepared high school graduates.

How Are They Doing?

Urban minorities in larger numbers turn to community colleges as their point of access to higher education. At the same time, they come with severe academic deficiencies, ranging from basic skills to limited or inadequate backgrounds in math and science. Their aspirations for baccalaureate degrees are not much different from the aspirations of their counterparts in suburban colleges. Yet because of their educational background, they are more likely to be advised to enter a vocational program rather than a transfer program. Concurrently, the transfer function of many community colleges, including those in urban areas, appears endangered. At particular risk is the survival of a coherent two-year sequence for the declining number of full-time students interested in earning a baccalaureate degree.

Questions of the effectiveness of community college transfer programs and of attrition patterns for students may need to be reexamined on the basis of a recent longitudinal study of the City University of New York. In that study, open admissions students graduated at a rate of 16 percent after four years, another 16 percent after five years, and an additional 11 percent after 11 years, producing a total graduation rate of 43 percent (Lavin, Murtha, and Kaufman 1984). Regularly admitted students, in contrast, graduated at accelerated rates during the early years of the study, followed by a distinct plateauing effect in later years during which graduation rates for both groups tended to converge. Perhaps the most important observation involves the persistence and courage observed among those who managed to balance their problems and challenges of life for as long as 11 years in their quest for a degree. Clearly, research on attrition needs to be redesigned to accommodate longer time frames than those used in the past to assess the performance of traditional, full-time students.

How Can They Improve Practice?
Certain policies and activities enhance the transfer of community college students: (1) university scholarships for transfer students; (2) reserved dorm space for mid-year transfers; (3) coordination of veterans' benefits; (4) joint faculty events and counseling exchanges; and (5) dual enrollment, whereby a transfer student is paired with a peer for easier acclimatization at no greater cost than single enrollment (Breyer 1982). Inevitably, where a transfer is successful, a strong articulation agreement is both present and honored.

Within the City University of New York, the Task Force on Student Retention and Academic Performance (1984) advanced the following recommendations: (1) improved admission procedures with special attention to the direct admission of qualifed late applicants; (2) intensive counseling programs; (3) block programs and paired courses for underprepared students; (4) detection and dismissal of students who fail after repeated attempts to complete remedial work; (5) early warning of students in academic difficulty with prompt administrative followup; and (6) on-line information systems to help in counseling students with academic difficulties. These recommendations appear equally relevant to urban universities and community colleges throughout the nation.

Some of the strategies being implemented in urban community colleges include university courses offered on community college campuses, concurrent enrollment at both universities and community colleges, improved orientation programs, peer counselors, mentors, special courses, and outside speakers used as role models to assist students in defining career objectives and in developing educational plans for their achievement (Schaier-Pelleg 1984).

It will take time to deal with issues related to the quality of urban secondary schools and the socioeconomic status of those who attend them. The existence of problems that lie beyond the immediate influence of community colleges and universities should not, however, be used as a rationale for avoiding institutional action. As in most areas of human endeavor, we know more about improving opportunities for urban minorities than we are currently using. Colleges and universities with a strong commitment to promoting equal educational opportunity have the means at their disposal to improve outcomes over those currently being achieved.

ADVISORY BOARD

CONSULTING EDITORS

Ernest A. Lynton
Commonwealth Professor and Senior Associate
Center for the Study of Policy and the Public Interest
University of Massachusetts

Gerald W. McLaughlin
Institutional Research and Planning Analysis
Virginia Polytechnic Institute and State University

Theodore J. Marchese
Vice President
American Association for Higher Education

L. Jackson Newell
Professor and Dean
University of Utah

Harold Orlans
Office of Programs and Policy
United States Civil Rights Commission

Richard H. Quay
Social Science Librarian
Miami University

John E. Stecklein
Professor of Educational Psychology
University of Minnesota

James H. Werntz, Jr.
Vice Chancellor for Academic Affairs
University of North Carolina

Donald Williams
Professor of Higher Education
University of Washington

CONTENTS

FOREWORD

The facts are stark. In the next two decades, the white population in the United States will decrease and minority populations, especially Hispanics, will increase dramatically. A disproportionate number of minorities reside in urban areas. To avoid greater division between the educated white majority and uneducated minorities, there must be a concerted effort to improve the articulation of junior and community college students to 4-year colleges and universities. This report addresses that challenge.

Why does more attention need to be focused on urban students? Traditionally, they have had lower attendance rates and a higher dropout rate than their suburban counterparts. The significance of a baccalaureate degree cannot be underestimated—it helps improve job prospects, earning power, productivity, and self-image; in short, it provides life options. Failure to address the urban student problem will further exacerbate societal fragmentation. The improved performance of urban students should become a national social objective as well as an educational one. Otherwise, urban populations will continue to have some of the highest unemployment and underemployment rates in the country.

Another aim of this report is to help urban college administrators and professors look at their roles with fresh eyes. For a variety of reasons, urban high schools and colleges have tended to channel students into terminal programs, rather than taking extra effort to encourage and teach them at least the basic skills. Counselors who routinely advise minority students to participate in work-experience programs illustrate the overall callous attitude and further limit student options. Although this issue has wide-ranging ramifications, educators have a responsibility to change the treatment of urban minority students, who often come from lower-income families.

The authors, Louis Bender, professor of higher education at Florida State University, and Richard Richardson, Jr., professor of higher education at Arizona State University, are principal investigators in a Ford Foundation-supported study called "Improving Transfer Opportunities for Urban Students." This report grew out of that study.

This sixth report in the 1985 ASHE-ERIC series contains some troubling information. Recognizing that the plight of urban students is much different from that of the suburban

---

student can go a long way towards preparing administrators, counselors, and professors to help them. Many of the problems facing urban colleges foreshadow issues in all academe. For example, the older, nontraditional student who may also have job and family responsibilities first appeared in the urban institution. So too did the student whose choice of major was linked to job security. It is clear that all colleges and universities must now seek solutions to these problems.

Jonathan D. Fife
Series Editor
Professor and Director
ERIC Clearinghouse on Higher Education
The George Washington University

ACKNOWLEDGEMENTS

The preparation of this report was supported by a grant from the Ford Foundation. Special thanks are owed to Alison Bernstein, Program Officer, for her support and counsel.

The manuscript was read by Richard Alfred, University of Michigan; and by David Leslie of Florida State University. Both made helpful comments that were incorporated into the final draft.

Several graduate assistants were involved. At Arizona State Kathleen Kistler, Virginia Stahl, Naomi Johnson and Eleanor Strang were particularly helpful. Susan Chalfonte-Thomas and Cheryl Blanco contributed at Florida State.

Last, but by no means least, the manuscript was typed—and retyped—by Dorla Nelson and Betty Bender.

To all of these individuals we express sincere appreciation.

INTRODUCTION

An unusual characteristic of American higher education is the emphasis placed on freedom of movement between institutions having significantly different missions, program emphases, and expectations for students' performance. Implicit within this arrangement for achieving equal educational opportunity has been the assumption that students who begin in an open access institution will, if successful, be able to move to institutions providing different and more advanced opportunities. Over the years, the success of efforts to achieve articulation between quite different institutions has been studied many times. In general, such studies have indicated successful movement among institutions as well as less systematic and clearly defined paths than would be optimum for students' achievement of baccalaureate degrees.

At the same time, general studies of the effectiveness of the transfer function have given inadequate attention to urban areas. Those students who pose the greatest challenge to efforts aimed at equality of opportunity are disproportionately concentrated in cities. Simply stated, more poor people, more immigrants, and more minorities live in urban settings where those among the college-age population are still less than half as likely to enroll in college than their suburban counterparts. The problem is particularly urgent in center cities (College Entrance Examination Board 1981).

The demographic profile of American children now entering public schools makes it clear that the problems for urban colleges and universities will grow in magnitude and complexity in the years ahead. Following the baby boom in the 1950s and the early 1960s, the birth rate among whites dropped while remaining constant for minorities. A larger segment of those entering the school system will be minority. The profile shows further that poverty is increasing rather than diminishing, particularly among minority populations. One in five children in this country now lives below the poverty level, and the number of children raised in one-parent households has increased significantly (College Entrance Examination Board 1985; Feistritzer 1985). These trends will increase the percentages of nontraditional students seeking higher education in urban settings.

Educational opportunities in urban areas often are not equal to those in surrounding suburban and rural areas, at

Simply stated, more poor people, more immigrants and more minorities live in urban settings where . . . less than half [are] as likely to enroll in college than their suburban counterparts.

least in terms of institutions that are accessible to the poor. A recent study of the Chicago area (Orfield et al. 1984) discloses that city and suburban high schools are different worlds educationally, with wide gaps existing even within the city. Schools in areas populated by more affluent whites experience lower dropout rates and smaller class sizes. Moreover, they have more teachers and more specialists in key precollegiate subjects. In the minority areas of the city, schools lack even the basic essentials for college preparation, and those few students who do complete school operate far below grade level.

The differences in precollegiate preparation quite naturally lead to differential access to opportunities at the baccalaureate level. The nature of the problem was well stated at the 1984 joint meeting of the American Council on Education and the National Association of State Universities and Land-Grant Colleges. The need to improve access for minorities is one major unfinished piece of business that lies before all of American higher education (Heller 1984). The third annual status report on minorities in higher education (Wilson and Melandez 1984) points out the continuing underrepresentation of blacks, Hispanics, and native Americans in four-year institutions and the proportional declines in enrollment experienced among blacks since 1976. Of most concern, though, has been the significant loss in share of degrees received. The report concludes by noting that minorities are more likely to leave secondary school before graduation. Those who do enter postsecondary education are less likely to complete a degree; of those who attend college, approximately half will attend two-year rather than four-year schools, despite roughly equivalent expectations for a baccalaureate degree (College Entrance Examination Board 1985).

The public urban university and the community college, most of which have been established during the past quarter century, have been expected to serve the urban poor. This report focuses on the progress such institutions have made in addressing access in the urban context. In making this assessment, the authors have chosen to focus on achievement of the baccalaureate degree that serves as gatekeeper to the professions. Career-related work in two-year colleges admittedly is important, although the tendency exists for minority students to be underrepresented in the more selective and generally higher-demand allied health programs within the two-year college.

In brief, minorities have increased their access to post-secondary education, but such access has been primarily through two-year institutions and preponderantly through those located in urban areas. Astin (1982) is among the researchers who have been most critical of the dispropor-tionate concentration of minority students in institutions with the fewest resources, particularly in community colleges. Noting that the hierarchical systems in some states are supported by a policy of selective admissions that forces minority students into community colleges, he concludes that the educational opportunities provided to the typical minority student and the typical white student are not equivalent. Olivas (1979) expresses similar concern. Among blacks, 37 percent of all full-time students are enrolled in two-year colleges. For Hispanics and American Indians, the comparable figures are 45 percent and 48 per-cent. In contrast, only 27 percent of full-time white stu-dents are enrolled in two-year institutions. To a consider-able degree then, the problem is one of minority access to four-year institutions.

Reasons for the existence of the problem are not hard to discover. Nationally, 13 percent of the students participat-ing in the Cooperative Institutional Research Program (CIRP) indicate they need remedial assistance in English, while 23 percent make the same statement about mathe-matics (Cohen and Brawer 1982a). The figures for urban areas, with their heavy concentrations of minority stu-dents, are much higher, ranging up to 85 to 90 percent for institutions that draw students predominantly from inner city populations. While declining enrollments may have blurred the distinctions between four-year comprehensive colleges and community colleges, research-oriented univer-sities continue their resistance to devoting any substantial percentage of total effort to remedial work (Riesman 1981). Where such work is provided, the tendency is to isolate it from mainstream institutional activity (Richardson, Mar-tens, and Fisk 1981).

Thus, it falls to community colleges in urban areas to serve as the point of access for those minorities who do not rank in the top quintile of their high school graduating classes. Even ranking in that top quintile is relatively meaningless for those who attend some inner city high schools. As a consequence, community colleges are inundated with underprepared students. At Miami-Dade, for example, two-thirds of all entering students tested are deficient in reading, writing, or mathematics; among blacks, more than 90 percent are deficient in one of these skills and two-thirds are deficient in all three (McCabe 1982–83).

Urban public universities also provide educational opportunities to a heterogeneous clientele, including underrepresented and underprepared students. They enroll a significant part, if not a majority, of their student body from the local community (Smartt 1981). In many states, however, these institutions are under pressure to raise admission requirements and to reduce the amount of remedial work they offer (Southern Regional Education Board 1983). If the problems of underrepresentation of minorities are to be addressed under such circumstances, it will be important to strengthen the transfer function of community colleges and to reduce the barriers to successful transfer resulting from some of the practices of four-year institutions.

Despite the tendency of urban community colleges to emphasize vocational programs, urban students in general and minority students in particular express the desire to earn a baccalaureate degree in percentages not very different from their suburban and rural counterparts. In fact, a good deal of the support for transfer education comes from students and from leaders of minority groups who object to the concentration on nonacademic programs, both remedial and vocational, in colleges with large minority enrollments (Lombardi 1979). Among the obstacles all students face in transferring are loss of credits, remedial work required to cope with studies, and a greater length of time to complete the degree than typically required for native students (Cohen and Brawer 1981–82). One important thesis to be explored in this report involves the extent to which these conditions are better or worse in urban areas. Some evidence suggests that conditions may be worse. Sponsored by the Ford Foundation, institutions in the urban college and university network have identified the following persistent obstacles to offering educational opportunities to students from nontraditional backgrounds: (1) adverse demographic and economic trends; (2) lack of funds to support necessary programs and staff; (3) deficiencies in staff skills or attitudes; (4) community apathy and even hostility; (5) unhealthy competition among institutions for students and resources; (6) outdated institutional missions; (7) public misperception of institutional purpose, resulting in a distorted image; (8) poor planning and management at every level; and (9) organizational inflexibilities (Schaier-Pelleg 1984).

Concern about the quality of educational opportunity offered to students in urban areas is not new. More than a decade ago, the Carnegie Commission (1972) recommended that the major responsibility for increasing access to higher education be through community colleges, with comprehensive colleges taking the lead in expanding access to upper division work. The commission also advised four-year colleges and universities to reexamine admission policies and practices so as to matriculate at least some portion of their entering students on a flexible basis. Many public universities now have policies for admitting "differentially qualified" students as some part of the total entering class, generally not exceeding 10 percent. Significantly, the proportion of minority students in many urban universities hovers around 10 percent and recently has been declining.

An acceptable definition of an urban university has yet to be coined, but Waetjen and Muffo (1983) have suggested a continuum to explain the array of missions reflected in America's urban institutions. At one extreme is the traditional university that emulates the residential model and accepts its urban location as a matter of coincidence. At the other end of the continuum is the socially oriented university, which has been described as a social service agency serving as a center of social action in addressing the problems of the urban environment (Berube 1978). At the center of the continuum are those "transitional institutions" that may go in either direction. Urban research universities, by virtue of their mission and the caliber of the professionals they attract, are pulled toward the traditional model. Comprehensive colleges and universities are closer to the center of the continuum, while the role of the socially oriented institution most nearly fits the comprehensive community college. In many respects, this division of responsibilities can be regarded as admirable. The key to success in providing equitable opportunities for baccalaureate achievement in the urban setting, however, relies upon the effectiveness of articulation arrangements among the three segments.

In recognition of the importance of these links, the Ford Foundation provided identical grants to Arizona State University and to Florida State University to conduct research in eight urban areas describing institutional or state policies and practices that either facilitate or impede attainment of the baccalaureate degree. The research project has been designed cooperatively with representatives from participating community colleges and universities working closely with principal investigators in the development of procedures for collecting and analyzing data. One of the agreements under which the project is being conducted is that institutional representatives will verify the accuracy of the descriptive information and participate in the development of research implications. The review of the literature reported in this monograph was completed as one phase of the project.

The cities in the Ford project include Chicago, Cleveland, Dallas, Miami, Newark, Philadelphia, Phoenix, and St. Louis. The study focuses on urban institutions. To be designated as urban, the institution has to enroll a significant proportion of minority students. None of the community colleges enrolled less than 20 percent minorities, excluding Asiatics. With the exception of two institutions, minority representation in community colleges ranged from 38 to 95 percent. The institutions that grant baccalaureate degrees were selected because they serve the same major metropolitan area as the urban community college and because they are the most important recipient of its transfer students. With the exception of one comprehensive university serving a predominantly minority student population, the minority enrollment in participating universities ranged from 10 to 15 percent.

While this review is not intended as a report of research findings from the current project, experiences in these eight cities during the past 18 months have inevitably shaped the perspective from which the literature is interpreted. Where studies of single cities are emphasized, it is because the findings are consistent with the experiences of the authors.

The next section of this report focuses on the characteristics and aspirations of urban students. In this report, the term "urban students" means those who attend public colleges and universities that have heavy concentrations of minority students and are located in metropolitan areas. The term "minority students" is used where available research information identifies such students as a subset of the urban student population and permits discussion of their needs and aspirations. Where data have not been disaggregated by racial status, the more inclusive term, urban student, is used.

The third section of this report focuses on public colleges and universities in the urban setting. The fourth section addresses outcomes in terms of the performance of urban students in public institutions, and the final section examines some of the strategies that have been suggested for overcoming barriers to urban students' attaining baccalaureate degrees.

The demographic profile of American children has changed dramatically since 1970. While the white population has increased by 6 percent, its percentage of total population dropped from 87.4 percent in 1970 to 83.2 percent in 1980. Blacks, the second largest racial group in the country, now represent about 12 percent of the total population. More important, this trend takes on special significance for the inner city, where 54.2 percent of all black children in this nation live. The fastest growing minority group includes persons of Hispanic origin. And they too are disproportionately located in the inner city (Feistritzer 1985).

The demographics of emerging student populations underscore the need for examining postsecondary education in urban areas. Twenty-eight percent of all white Americans (Caucasians) are 18 or younger. For blacks, the comparable figure is 37 percent, for Hispanics, 42 percent. Seventy-five percent of white youth aged 18 and 19 have graduated from high school, in comparison with 57 percent of the black population and 54 percent of Hispanics. Among the population as a whole, only 17 percent of Hispanics 18 or older have attended college. For blacks, the figure is 20 percent, for whites, 32 percent (Boyer 1981; College Entrance Examination Board 1985).

Among the population as a whole, only 17 percent of Hispanics 18 or older have attended college.

An influx of over 4 million foreign-born immigrants to this country occurred between the 1970 and the 1980 census. A large proportion of such immigrants have limited ability to speak English. Again, it is the inner city educational institutions that are confronted with large populations having language-related educational disadvantages. Spanish is the predominant language of the foreign-born immigrants, but many other language groups are also represented (National Center for Education Statistics 1984a).

The Hispanic population cannot easily be categorized because of its diversity. Based on 1980 data, a recent study of Americans of Hispanic heritage reported Mexican-Americans had the lowest proportion of students in college, while Cuban-Americans were closer to white Americans in income and college attendance patterns. The Puerto Rican population had a higher college attendance rate than Mexican-Americans, although their family income generally was lower. The remaining group, a combination of other Latinos, tended to have higher college attendance rates and family incomes (Lee 1984).

Financial Perspective

The 1973 U.S. poverty level of 11.1 percent grew to 15.2 percent in 1983; the level for whites increased from 8.4 percent to 12 percent, for blacks from 31.4 percent to 35.7 percent, and for Hispanics from 21.9 percent to 28.4 percent. For black children, the increase was from 40.6 percent to 46.3 percent and for Hispanics, from 27.8 percent to 37.8 percent. One-third of all children living in inner cities are poor, but over half (57 percent) of the poor are black (College Entrance Examination Board 1985; Feistritzer 1985).

Black and Hispanic Americans represent a larger proportion of families with dependent children, a condition not usually reflected in the general description of poverty. Their income typically supports more people than that of white families, and even slight shifts in financial support can therefore change college attendance patterns. Recent studies suggest it is more difficult economically to enroll in college now than five years ago. Minorities have actually lost resources during this period, both in the form of family income and in student aid dollars (College Entrance Examination Board 1985; Lee 1984).

On average, black and Hispanic students have received more federal student aid than whites. In the fall of 1983, black students averaged $1,854 in grants and loans, Hispanic students $1,554, and white students $1,260. These data, calculated from responses by first-time, full-time freshmen in the annual freshmen norms sample of the Cooperative Institutional Research Progam (CIRP), are consistent with the income patterns between minority and white families (Astin et al. 1983).

In New Jersey, the average cost for a residential student attending a state college in 1984–85 was $5,394. With maximum Pell, Tag, and Equal Opportunity Fund awards totaling $3,688 students still needed to come up with $1,706 from other sources (New Jersey Department of Higher Education 1984). Clearly, part of the now increasing discrepancy between participation rates for minority and nonminority students can be attributed to the declining value of available student aid (College Entrance Examination Board 1985).

Educational Equality

Access as a goal of American higher education is generally accepted as an achievement of the early 1970s; however, less attention has been given to equity in educational services and the quality of such services. Equality cannot be claimed if, by accident of birth, individuals are confronted by environmental constraints that limit the nature and scope of educational and personal development, yet youth in central cities are often confronted with schooling that is clearly inferior to that experienced by youth attending suburban schools. Minorities are disproportionately more likely than whites to be enrolled in special education and vocational education programs. They are less likely to be involved in academic programs or programs for the gifted and talented. Among the college bound, minorities are more likely to have experienced fewer years of course work in mathematics and physical science than their white counterparts. Even the content of courses varies significantly. A comparison among white and black seniors who had taken three years of math indicated whites were more likely to have taken algebra, geometry, trigonometry, or calculus, while black seniors were more likely to have taken general math or business math (College Entrance Examination Board 1985).

Low-income students in predominantly minority schools have less access to microcomputers or teachers trained in computer uses than students at predominantly majority schools. Even differences in computer applications have been noted. Minority schools are more likely to use computers for drill and practice, in contrast to programming and concept development more typically found in classrooms of majority schools (Winkler et al. 1984).

The less challenging educational programs of the minority schools are less likely to contribute to the development of higher-order cognitive skills and abilities than the educational programs of majority schools. Although black students from urban schools made strong gains in mathematics and reading scores during the 1970s, much of the credit has been given to federally funded compensatory programs that are now being cut or eliminated. It is reasonable to question whether current policy trends will reverse the improved educational attainment levels of minorities and their improved participation in scientific and technical fields of study. Current evidence suggests participation has declined in addition to continuing problems with the achievement of a degree (College Entrance Examination Board 1985).

Aspirations

Despite the tendency for urban community colleges to concentrate on occupational education and social services, the degree intentions of urban students are very similar to those of the population in general. In one nationwide survey administered in public two-year colleges having at least one-third minority enrollment, more than 52 percent of all respondents claimed preparation for transfer as their primary reason for attending college. In contrast, 41 percent indicated they were preparing to enter a specific occupation. In all, more than 74 percent of the respondents expressed the intent to obtain a B.A. or higher degree at some point in their lives (Bensimon and Riley 1984). These figures are substantially higher than those reported in an earlier study for the California system as a whole (Hunter and Sheldon 1981). The figures suggest the transfer function is as important in urban settings as in suburban or rural schools.

Despite the importance of the transfer function, no one can state with accuracy how many students transfer from community colleges to four-year colleges and universities (Cohen 1979). Despite the absence of reliable data permitting comparisons across states, some have suggested that the transfer function has declined in importance and effectiveness among community colleges in general. In Illinois, baccalaureate-oriented enrollment in community colleges peaked in 1975, following a period of uninterrupted growth. By 1979, baccalaureate-oriented enrollment had declined almost 14 percent. During the same time period, undeclared enrollment increased by more than 233 percent (Smith 1980, p. 253). The problem of transfer decline may be particularly acute in urban settings (Kissler 1982; Lombardi 1979). Some also have asserted that community colleges "cool out" students who otherwise would have succeeded in a senior institution (Astin 1982; Duran 1983). Community colleges do in fact alter students' aspirations for transfer by encouraging them to enroll in vocational programs rather than transferring to four-year institutions, but the process does not work smoothly (London 1978). Students are quite anxious over the consequences of both failure and success, and their frustration is evident in their absenteeism and their relationships with teachers and with each other (London 1978).

Just as minority students are concentrated disproportionately in urban two-year institutions, their numbers in urban universities exceed those on nonurban campuses. In one 10-state sample, the median rate of attendance for blacks in nonurban universities was slightly over 4 percent. For urban universities in those same states, the median black enrollment was almost 9 percent (Smartt 1981). Within urban universities, many of the minority students are transfers from community colleges. In Florida, 76 percent of the minorities within the state university system began their education in a community college (Florida Board of Regents 1985). Not only do community college transfers constitute a majority among the minority students enrolled in urban universities but they also represent the greatest potential for future growth.

Currently, the concern is more with graduation than with participation rates. A variety of sources suggest that minority students, and especially black males, may be losing ground in the proportion of baccalaureate degrees they are earning (College Entrance Examination Board 1985; Wilson and Melandez 1984). Part of the problem unquestionably relates to the way such rates are calculated. Those who begin college with academic deficiencies and limited economic resources require more than the normal four- or five-year span to complete degrees. Studies that use five-year cutoffs distort the picture of graduation reality, just as policies that cut off financial assistance after five years penalize both open access institutions and the students they attract (Lavin, Murtha, and Kaufman 1984). In the City University of New York (CUNY), a number of reasons were given for the longer time to graduation of open admission students: the need to register for remedial courses offering little or no credit, the requirement to work full time while attending college, and "stopping out" for family problems (Lavin, Murtha, and Kaufman 1984). As a related CUNY report suggests, "Our students do not live in dormitories isolated from reality by monthly allowances and clean laundry from provident parents. They are not isolated by the ivy-covered buildings from the shocks and assaults of urban life'' (Task Force 1984, p. 2). Such students cannot reasonably be expected to conform to traditional college patterns, ''but we do them a disservice not to maintain standards [that] make their certificates and diplomas worth printing'' (p. 2).

PUBLIC COLLEGES AND UNIVERSITIES IN URBAN AREAS

Colleges and universities located in the inner cities of major metropolitan areas have a number of common challenges. Their student bodies include working adults, many minorities, poor people, persons with low levels of educational preparedness, and, increasingly, immigrants whose native language is not English. Many of these institutions are committed to a policy of open admissions, and the remainder tend not to be highly selective in admission. They do not draw many students from beyond a commuting range of the institution. As institutions, they are tied organically to their cities and the problems of people who reside there (Cafferty and Spangenberg 1983).

The problems of urban-oriented institutions include institutional funding, student poverty, high attrition, school system failures, confused missions, an overvaluing of traditional ways at the expense of local community needs, an undervaluing of institutional cooperation, and failure to communicate. Their single greatest problem is the need of their students for help with basic skills (Cafferty and Spangenberg 1983). The problems of the urban environment are shared by community colleges and universities.

Their single greatest problem is the need of their students for help with basic skills.

Urban Community Colleges

The American Association of Community and Junior Colleges directory for 1984 lists the full- and part-time 1983 fall enrollment for its 1,219 member colleges. Public two-year institutions reported 4,799,768 enrollees. Urban community colleges accounted for over 60 percent of student enrollments, and they typically played a dominant role in formulating policy and overall direction of the community college system in each of the states. Because of their size, urban institutions enjoy a state and national reputation for leadership. Trustees and presidents of these institutions are regularly found on commissions, councils, and task forces, whether created by legislative or professional organizations.

Strategic to understanding the perspective of this report is the fact that most urban institutions are multicampus systems, with units serving different areas within the college's jurisdiction. Many of these multicampus organizations are known as districts, and various degrees of autonomy can be found among the individual campuses of such districts. The college or campus serving the inner city will be quite different in purposes, programs, and students from a unit located on the fringes of the city or in the suburbs.

The inner city campus of the urban community college district often suffers from an image problem traceable to attitudes toward the socioeconomic status of its clientele. Faculty sometimes shun assignments to a city campus in favor of assignment to a suburban setting. Educational programs at the urban campus are often less comprehensive and place greater emphasis on remedial programs, occupational programs, and community service. They may offer only meager transfer options. Even the physical facilities of downtown campuses sometimes reflect a lower priority than suburban campuses. Comparisons of space allocations, maintenance, and even laboratory and instructional equipment may reveal differences in priorities and direction. For these reasons, it is difficult to generalize about urban community colleges without disaggregating the individual campuses and the diverse communities they serve.

A recent study (Orfield et al. 1984) provides a critical view of the educational opportunities provided by community colleges in the city of Chicago. Within the city, these colleges are the most important resource for black and Hispanic students, but they have only marginal importance to whites. Actual course offerings are narrower in some fields in the city colleges than in their suburban counterparts. Students are viewed as being less prepared for transfer by receiving institutions. An inverse relationship exists between the responsiveness of colleges to students' requests for information and the socioeconomic status of the students served. Colleges serving the poorest students are the least likely to provide adequate information. The general conclusion of the report is that the higher education system within the metropolitan Chicago area functions in many ways to reflect, and sometimes reinforce, underlying inequalities. Other writers, including those from within community colleges, have been critical of the quality of programs and services received by minority students. Another writer notes Hispanic students have flocked to such institutions, believing their needs would be well served, but in general the services have not lived up to the promise (de los Santos 1980).

At inner city campuses where the percentage of underprepared students is high, transfer education offerings decline. As a result, advanced courses in most transfer subjects cannot be offered each semester and at best may be offered every second or third semester. The flight of white students from inner city schools is reflected in the composition of students attending the more urban centers of multicampus districts. As one result, some campuses offer only a semblance of transfer education (Lombardi 1979). In the Chicago study, city colleges offered on the average 42 percent of their advertised curriculum, in contrast to 76 percent for suburban colleges. The interpretation of open admissions used by many urban community colleges also results in many underprepared students' entering transfer courses. It is difficult to keep course content and assignments at baccalaureate-equivalent levels when the number of academically prepared students represents only a small fraction of the total students enrolled in a class (Kissler 1982).

Assessment and placement practices in community colleges are often attributed to state laws' requirements for open admissions. Generally, however, the effort to make classes accessible to students who lack basic skills reflects more the absence of acceptable alternatives than state requirements. In Illinois, for example, state law provides that students allowed entry to college transfer programs should have ability and competence similar to those possessed by students admitted to state universities for similar programs. Recently, community colleges and universities in the Chicago area have begun assessing entering students' reading competencies and identifying their reading intensive courses, and students are not permitted to enroll in the reading intensive courses until their reading deficiencies have been corrected. Most states have open admission requirements for community colleges similar to those for Illinois. Little evidence suggests community colleges could not legally require students to correct deficiencies before enrolling in transfer courses.

Of course, most community colleges still practice advisory placement and do not assess all entering students. One recent study of a comprehensive urban community college found an absence of procedures for placing students accurately in terms of entering qualifications, as well as a lack of literacy standards for completion of the degree. Many advanced courses did not carry prerequisites.

Course completion rates were low. Student advising was minimal, partly as a consequence of the employment of large numbers of part-time faculty (Richardson, Fisk, and Okun 1983).

A narrowing of the curriculum combined with low completion rates have led some writers to conclude that community colleges do not really serve the interests of students coming directly from high school to pursue careers requiring the baccalaureate degree (Astin 1977; Breneman and Nelson 1981). Despite these criticisms, it is difficult to view the role of urban community colleges in other than sympathetic terms. They do confront enormous problems. For many of the students they serve, they are the only alternative. Even those who criticize urban community colleges note that such institutions place considerably more emphasis on establishing a supportive environment for minority students than do their baccalaureate-oriented counterparts. In addition, urban community colleges have the significant advantage of being able to provide underprepared students with longer periods of time to remedy deficiencies. The weight of evidence suggests that students who complete two years in a community college perform reasonably well after they transfer.

Urban Universities
Before examining more closely some of the concerns that have been raised about the comparative standards maintained by community colleges and universities, one needs to consider the role of the urban university. The interactions between public universities and their metropolitan regions are so diverse that no single definition or classification exists. Numerous attempts have been made to study these missions and interactions. The National Association of State Universities and Land-Grant Colleges found it necessary to establish a separate division for its urban members to consider their special concerns, but no single articulated definition has been produced by even this body.

Despite the absence of a definition of what constitutes an urban university, writers generally agree on their responsibility for contributing to the economic development of the areas they serve through research and technical assistance. Urban universities located in emerging and growing cities typically establish themselves as part of the resource base used by planners, developers, and promoters within city government, chambers of commerce, or business and community influentials. Those urban universities located in the older, more mature cities, on the other hand, typically carve out a comparable role in the areas of revitalization, renewal, and leadership (Grobman and Sanders 1984).

Some have argued that the environment of each urban public university is so special that functional distinctions must be made. The "growth" cities in the sun belt are often contrasted with the "mature" cities in the Northeast or frost belt. Such a difference is true only in the short term, however, and the long-range conditions from the perspective of the urban university will be more similar than different (Rudnick 1983).

Urban public universities often are viewed as committed to the goal of achieving the traditional residential university model at the expense of the challenges, clienteles, and needs of the cities where they are located. Calls have been sounded for curriculum reform as well as for reappraisal of relationships of the urban university with the other parts of the educational system. Yet many urban universities evidence concern about their role and status in American higher education.

These urban presidents and chancellors believe that at the multicampus system level and beyond, there is an unfortunate perception that an institution cannot truly be a university and still deal with problems and obligations presented by the inner city. The implication, therefore, is that urban public universities are "lesser" entities (Rudnick 1983, p. 10).

While calls have been sounded for an institution committed to approach urban problems in the same manner that land-grant universities deal with rural problems (Carnegie Commission 1972; Rudnick 1983), universities serving an urban clientele probably are better described as American universities in the urban context. Such institutions reflect their location by providing programs that serve the basic educational needs of place-bound and traditionally underrepresented clienteles (Smartt 1981). University officials are often unwilling to showcase their special programs for the urban underprepared, however. They do not want to emphasize programs for weak students at the same time they are involved in activities designed to upgrade their image as research institutions. They are also concerned that serving underprepared students might come to be seen as a principal component in the mission of an urban institution. In brief, while urban universities are not opposed to helping the underprepared, the urban mission is more commonly expressed in terms of curricula and research focused on urban topics and problems (Rudnick 1983).

Even though urban universities may choose not to emphasize the work they do with underprepared students, it is clear that they, as well as their student populations, are different from residential universities in suburban or rural settings. In particular, urban universities place greater emphasis on flexible scheduling of classes and services to meet the needs of part-time students. They have more structured forms of support services, and they are likely to have a very large commitment to professional and technical programs as contrasted with undergraduate arts and sciences. Given these characteristics, urban universities may be placed at a disadvantage by state formula funding that fails to give adequate attention to the relatively high cost of the additional services and professional program emphases. The problem is exacerbated by the fact that many urban universities continue to grow while the state systems of which they are a part have entered a period of decline. Under such circumstances, great temptation exists at the state policy level to limit the development of new programs in urban settings to avoid taking resources from a flagship campus (Rudnick 1983).

The relative youth of most urban universities has contributed to some of their ambiguous mission. The faculty are often graduates of the nation's most prestigious universities with academic backgrounds that stressed traditional scholarly research over teaching and service. It is not unusual for faculty to feel at odds with the priorities of the urban university for technical and professional programs and for the teaching requirements involved in serving urban students. Applied research and technical assistance to the urban community can be threatening to those conditioned to expect the more traditional forms of research. Professors may also find it difficult to accommodate the cultural differences represented among their students (Rud-nick 1983).

Urban University–Community College Relations
Urban universities suffer from some of their own image problems and typically do not perceive an improvement in the situation by linking themselves more closely with community colleges. To some degree, the two institutions compete, and the competition is most noticeable when urban universities are essentially open admissions institutions. Because of the large number of community colleges created during the past 25 years, it is easy to overlook the role of urban universities in accommodating increased enrollment in metropolitan areas. In reality, of some 15 large urban universities in the South, all but one were created or made a free standing unit of the state system within the past 25 years (Smartt 1981). It is not surprising, therefore, that in many urban areas community colleges and universities perceive themselves to be actively competing for some of the same students, particularly among better-prepared high school graduates. This competition does nothing to improve the already limited disposition to cooperate.

Another problem is grading standards. A number of studies have found that university and community college faculty differ significantly in their orientation toward grading. The heterogeneous student clientele and the community college's emphasis on nurturing lead to the adoption of self-referenced norms, which tends to inflate grades awarded in the community college. In part, transfer shock results from students' moving from the self-referenced grading systems of the community college to the more norm-referenced grading systems of the university (Geisinger, Wilson, and Naumann 1980).

The problem may be particularly acute in the areas of mathematics and science. Although community college and university texts in the state of California cover the same topics, for example, they do not do so at the same academic levels (Russell and Perez 1980). Two reasons are likely for the differences: The mixing of transfer and non-transfer students in community colleges leads to lower levels of instruction, which are detrimental to the achievement of transfers, and in community colleges, depth is sacrificed for breadth (Russell and Perez 1980). Other differences cause problems for transfer students: differing calendar systems, size of campus, amount of faculty/student interaction, level of competition, withdrawal policies, and curriculum and pedagogy (Kissler 1981).

Regardless of where the articulation problem is studied, results appear similar. The documentation of significant barriers to successful transfer in such well-articulated systems as California and the City University of New York suggests that in other urban areas, where structural arrangements separate rather than link two- and four-year institutions and where little or no attention has been given to promoting cooperation between community colleges and universities, the problem is likely to be substantially more serious.

Given this background, it is particularly interesting to note the difficulties identified by CUNY's Task Force on Student Retention and Academic Performance, perhaps the one place in the country where the smallest number of problems from an organizational perspective ought to exist, because CUNY's two-year and four-year institutions have been an integral part of the same system. The task force identified the following seven problems within the system: (1) inadequate means of informing and advising students on appropriate programs and supplementary services; (2) programs for students for whom English is a second language; (3) underprepared freshmen and the wastefulness of students' repeating remedial courses with little chance of progress; (4) lack of faculty and administrative involvement in coordinated efforts at retention; (5) disparity in retention rates between professional programs and liberal arts programs; (6) the need to improve articulation between senior and community colleges; and (7) the demoralizing effect of inadequate or unsafe physical facilities and inadequate staff. The literature suggests the existence of such problems in other urban areas as well.

From the literature, it seems clear urban community colleges and universities are asked to deal with a seriously underprepared student population, a majority of whom have graduated from inadequate public schools. The issues are complex and the challenges formidable. While it is easy to be critical of current practice, a careful review of the circumstances suggests urban colleges and universities deserve considerable credit for coping with the problem as well as they do.

ASSESSING OUTCOMES

The phenomenon of transfer has received considerable attention in the years since community colleges were identified as the principal instrument for making the transition from meritocratic to universal opportunities for postsecondary education. Several of the best-designed research studies, including the landmark Knoell and Medsker study (1965), were completed before the changes in characteristics of community college students of the past decade. As a result, the findings of those studies may no longer be applicable, particularly in terms of the conditions that currently confront urban institutions, a majority of which had never graduated a class at the time data were collected for the Knoell and Medsker study.

While the newer studies for the most part are neither as comprehensive nor as well designed as several of the earlier studies, a considerable body of information exists about transfer in general, and an emerging body of literature deals specifically with issues related to minority students and transfer in urban areas. This part of the report discusses the attainment of degrees in two-year institutions, the numbers of students who transfer and at what stages in their college career, and what is known about the performance of transfers and their evaluation of the preparation provided by the community colleges from which they transferred.

While minorities constitute 20 percent of the total two-year enrollments they receive only 13 percent of the associate degrees in technology. . . .

Attainment of Associate Degrees

Some question exists about whether minorities attain associate degrees at levels that exceed by very much their proportional attainment of baccalaureate degrees. While one reference (Presley and Hagan 1981) suggests minority students are more likely to get associate degrees than nonminority students, other references indicate that the numbers of minorities receiving less than baccalaureate degrees are disappointing, indicating a lower success rate at the associate degree level for minority students. While minorities constitute 20 percent of the total two-year enrollments they receive only 13 percent of the associate degrees in technology and 15 percent of those in the transfer fields (Olivas 1979).

A related study cites high minority attrition rates in two-year colleges and indicates that white students, who account for approximately 77 percent of the total two-year college population, earned in excess of 84 percent of the associate degrees (Institute for the Study 1980). A third report, which excludes Puerto Rico from its calculations, indicates that within occupational programs in two-year colleges, white and Hispanic distributions resembled each other, except that Hispanics less frequently earned degrees in health services, paramedic, and natural science programs (College Entrance Examination Board 1981). Thus, the available evidence suggests minority students do not receive their proportional share of associate degrees, although the discrepancies appear less dramatic at this level than in the competition for baccalaureate degrees.

Focusing on the proportion of degrees earned overlooks one of the most important problems in the achievement of a degree from a two-year college. Many of the same community colleges that advocate open access, even to the extent of refusing to implement mandatory assessment and placement for seriously underprepared students, have admission standards for acceptance to some allied health programs that exceed those imposed in four-year institutions. Thus, at the same time community colleges are accused, with some justification, of tracking minority students into two-year vocational programs, they have waiting lists and selective admission policies for fields such as nursing, dental hygiene, and medical technology (Institute for the Study 1980). Substantial evidence also suggests that the use of waiting lists and highly selective admission standards for these more desirable programs actually acts to exclude minority students from enrollment (Olivas 1979).

Transfer
Turning from attainment of the associate degree to the major focus of this report, progress to the baccalaureate, one finds the first issue involves the percentages of students who actually transfer. From examination of a total degree credit enrollment, estimates of those who transfer from community colleges to universities range from about 5 to 15 percent. In California, fewer than one in ten community college students completes a transfer degree and then subsequently transfers to a four-year institution. Since the early 1970s, the community college students transferring to the University of California or California State University systems have been declining in absolute numbers as well as in percentage of total

enrollment (California Postsecondary Education Commission 1981). By comparing the number of associate in arts and science degrees awarded in 1970–71 with those awarded in 1977–78, Cohen and Brawer (1982a) noted the number of transfer degrees awarded in the later year had declined to 41 percent of the total, while the total number of transfer degrees had nonetheless increased from 145,000 to about 167,000. Their best estimate of the number of people moving on from two- to four-year institutions was about 5 percent of the total enrollment in any given year.

Observing that the transfer function in California and elsewhere has declined is not the same as stating that it is no longer important. Almost 60,000 students transfer to the University of California and California State University systems alone each year. Most who transfer continue to do well academically (Kissler 1982). In Florida, where a strong articulation agreement has been in effect, the transfer population is an increasing segment of the state university system, with 43,748 such students in 1983 (42.2 percent of all state university system undergraduates) in contrast to 39,470 in 1981 (Florida Department of Education 1984).

In attempting to explain the apparent declining importance of the transfer function, most writers cite the growing diversity of students with respect to age, ethnicity, readiness and ability to do college-level work, previous educational attainment, interest in academic goals, and in the objective being pursued (Knoell 1982). Community college leaders are quick to point out the changing nature of their student clientele—the growing numbers who are part time and those who are not interested in transferring or earning a degree. While critical of researchers who have attempted to provide answers to questions about transfers, at the same time they have difficulty describing why students enroll other than in terms of course placement. The number of those in transfer programs may decline to approximately 3 to 5 percent of total enrollments if the present trends continue in such states as California and Washington (Friedlander 1980).

Several conditions seem clear from the literature. Minority students depend heavily upon urban community colleges, where they are likely to constitute a disproportionate part of the nontraditional student population. Their numbers have already been thinned by higher-than-normal high school dropout rates. Those who attend community colleges express the aspiration to transfer at rates equal to or above their better prepared nonminority counterparts. Many enter with serious academic deficiencies as a consequence of their high school preparation. They enter a postsecondary environment where transfer is a diminishing part of the total enterprise. A relatively small proportion of those who attend will actually transfer, but even a small proportion of the massive community college enterprise translates into large numbers and, more important, includes a very significant part of all minority students working to attain baccalaureate degrees.

Performance
As far back as the Knoell and Medsker (1965) study, differences have been noted between grades earned in the community college and grades earned after transfer to a four-year institution. In the early studies, this difference was often labeled "transfer shock." More recent studies, however, contain blunt assertions of differences in academic standards (Bragg 1982; Jackson and Drakulich 1976). A study of Los Angeles City College transfers to California State University at Los Angeles reports that while the average pretransfer grade point average was the highest in 12 years, the posttransfer GPA was the lowest during the same period (Gold 1980). There can be little doubt about the decline in the academic performance of community college transfers (Kissler 1982). The same study produced substantial evidence that community college transfers perform less well than either native students or those who transfer from other four-year institutions. The evidence is not totally one sided, however. The Newark campus of Rutgers University, which has the largest transfer population of all Rutgers campuses, found transfer students in the College of Arts and Sciences were less frequently dismissed for academic reasons than the average for the college as a whole (Hosford 1983). A different study at Rutgers University reported that associate degree holders were more likely to graduate with a baccalaureate and to have a higher GPA than those who had not completed degree requirements before transfer (Armstrong and Oppenheimer 1981).

Where studies correct for students' aptitude and high

school performance, differences between the performance of transfers in contrast with that of native students tend to disappear (Richardson and Doucette 1980). Without correcting for students' aptitude, the magnitude of the difference in performance for students who transfer to urban universities from urban community colleges may be greater than the .50 drop in GPA that has often been described as the norm in the literature. A study of students transferring from Essex County College reports a decline in mean grade point average of .65 points (Jackson and Drakulich 1976).

The Ford Foundation study being conducted by Arizona State and Florida State universities found community college faculty fairly evenly divided in their opinions of the importance of earning the associate degree before transfer. On some campuses, faculty viewed the credential as meaningless, while on other campuses, the importance of the degree to a successful transfer was stressed. The importance attached to the degree appeared to be a function of whether it was emphasized by formal articulation agreements as a preferred credential. Where the degree was emphasized, the ratio of sophomore to freshman students for the campus was on the order of one-to-three or -four, significantly lower than the overall one-to-five ratio reported by the American Association of Community and Junior Colleges (Richardson and Bender 1985).

Transfers from four-year public and private institutions consistently outperform those from community colleges (Anderson and Beers 1980; Harmon 1976; Kissler, Lara, and Cardinal 1981). Even so, the performance of community college transfers is quite similar to the performance of transfers from four-year institutions and the performance of native students. Part of the difference in performance clearly relates to the higher percentages of minority and nontraditional students counted among the two-year college transfer population.

A comparison of CUNY regular students and open admissions students is instructive in understanding transfer performance in urban areas. In the CUNY senior colleges, 34 percent of regular students graduated after four years, another 19 percent graduated after five years, and an additional 9 percent took more than five years to earn the bachelor's degree, producing a total rate of graduation of 62 percent. In contrast, only 16 percent of open admissions

students earned degrees after four years, although another 16 percent graduated after five years and an additional 11 percent graduated after 11 years, producing a total graduation rate of 43 percent. Of particular interest was the fact that minorities needed additional time, both in the regular category and in the open admissions category. Initial racial differences in graduation rates at the end of five years were substantially reduced and in some cases even eliminated after 11 years (Lavin, Murtha, and Kaufman 1984).

In Chicago, an analysis conducted over a period of five years concluded degree attainment for blacks and Hispanics had declined in comparison with growth in their college-age population. Of particular concern was the fact that the number of degrees awarded to blacks declined as a function of their representation in the college-age cohort (Orfield et al. 1984). Of course, it must be noted that had the CUNY study limited its examination to a five-year period, the researchers would have reached conclusions similar to those of the Chicago study.

While the evidence is far from absolute, enough indicators suggest the need to qualify Astin's (1982) conclusion that all students, both minority and nonminority, have a better chance of earning a baccalaureate degree if they begin in a four-year college or university. Several studies suggest a relative advantage may accrue to some students attending a two-year institution initially. The difference appears to depend upon whether a student is academically underprepared. A five-year followup for the University of Missouri at St. Louis found that while retention rates for first-time freshmen were higher than for transfers, the cumulative percentage of graduates among transfer students was approximately double that of first-time freshmen (Avakian, MacKinney, and Allen 1982). Reflecting the urban status of the institution and the short time period of the study, graduation rates were low (15 percent for native freshmen and 25 percent for transfers). Of particular interest was the finding that the advantage in retention rates held by white first-time freshmen students over black students appeared to be less pronounced for transfer students. A study using the national longitudinal study of the high school class of 1972 discovered that community colleges increase the chances of some students for receiving a bachelor's degree (Breneman and Nelson 1981). These students "are more apt to have had a less academic high school experience, and, interestingly, to be black" (p. 92).

Support for this hypothesis is also available from a study by the Division of Institutional Research of the California State Universities and Colleges (1979). The five-year graduation rates of first-time freshmen for minorities as a group was 20.6 percent, compared to the rate for white, non-Hispanic students of 34.2 percent. The comparable three-year graduation rates for community college transfers over the same time period was 28.8 percent for minorities, compared to 38 percent for white, non-Hispanic students. These figures must be interpreted with caution because they were derived from students who attended college full time after graduating from high school in 1973. Nevertheless, they do suggest a differential impact for transfer in terms of graduation rates for minorities as compared with those for nonminorities.

A study conducted in Florida found retention among black community college transfers to be slightly less than the rate for white transfers systemwide. When examined over one- to three-year periods, it was found that the graduation rates for black community college transfer students have typically been between 10 to 12 percentage points below the 63 percent average success rate for whites (Florida Board of Regents 1984). This difference is very similar to the one found in California.

Finally, it may be important to note that success in graduating minorities at the baccalaureate degree level and success in passing externally mandated criterion examinations such as those for teacher certification may be two different phenomena. A recent review notes that although traditionally black colleges have a reputation for helping students through college and into successful careers, graduates of these institutions have had difficulty meeting new test score requirements for teacher certification (Dilworth 1984).

At the baccalaureate level, as in two-year institutions, minority students are disproportionately concentrated in such areas as education, social work, humanities, and the social sciences, so at least a part of the improved performance of minority students who transfer from community colleges may be a function of the programs into which they transfer. A trend toward minority transfers' seeking admission to limited access professional programs like business and computer science may be developing (Richardson and Bender 1985).

Information is needed about the extent to which two-year institutions prepare minorities to succeed in business and engineering baccalaureate programs. At least one source indicates that Hispanics more often earn degrees in social science fields and more whites enroll in scientific fields (College Entrance Examination Board 1981). A recent comparative study of black community college transfers with black native students at Florida State University found a greater proportion of black transfers choosing a mathematics major than natives (8.6 percent versus 5.7 percent), but more native black students (32.8 percent versus 21.8 percent) were enrolled in selected business majors than were black transfers. In examining patterns of major switching between the two groups, the same study found 47.1 percent of the transfers had switched, in contrast to 50.2 percent of the natives. An analysis of the direction of such switching found no significant difference between the two groups, with generally the same portions "switching up" to "tough" programs or "switching down" to less demanding programs (Milton, Levine, and Papagiannis 1984).

Leaving aside questions of academic preparation and performance, it seems clear that community colleges provide an environment that is more supportive of and responsive to minorities than do universities. In one study involving interviews with students who transferred to selective private institutions after beginning their postsecondary work in a community college, the researchers noted a recurrent theme: Community colleges, more than anything else in the students' experience, provided the opportunity to gain self-confidence. Students also commented on acquisition of basic skills important to success in college, but eventually all returned to a discussion of the positive feelings that community colleges evoked in them about themselves (Neumann and Reisman 1980).

In a study often cited by community college advocates as the type of research that ought to be done, students were asked to rate their preparation for transfer on a scale of "A" to "F." More than 70 percent rated their preparation as "A" or "B," 20 percent as "C," and a very small percentage as "D" or "F." Interestingly, in this same study, students did not rate their preparation for vocational training nearly as positively. Over 68 percent said their vocational courses were not helpful in getting a raise, and 74 percent made the same comment in terms of promotions. Perhaps most revealing, however, were the conclusions that vocational courses are often tangential to the central focus of a student's job and that 86 percent of those in the study indicated they were interested in receiving college credit for their work (Hunter and Sheldon 1981).

All in all, these results are not different from what would be expected. Students transfer from community colleges and perform successfully at universities. The longer they spend in a community college before transfer, the better they are likely to perform. Transfer students value the academic preparation they received in community colleges but are likely to emphasize the affective or supportive aspects of the community college environment rather than its academic rigor. In fact, students who begin their college experience in a university frequently "reverse transfer" to community colleges from which they may subsequently transfer back to the university, where they experience better success than they did on their first attempt (Gregg and Stroud 1977). The effects of community colleges on minority students, and particularly on those who are underprepared, may be more positive than the less caring environment of the university.

Despite this generally positive portrayal of the transfer function, reasons for concern remain. Attrition rates in community colleges are much higher even among comparable students than they are in universities. The enrollment of large numbers of underprepared students in transfer courses has raised questions about the academic rigor of these courses and perhaps contributed to a widening of the differences reported between the grade point average earned by students in a community college and the grade point average they subsequently earn after transferring to a university. Even though minority students may be as well or even somewhat better served in a community college than in a university, the performance of the system in terms of baccalaureate achievement for minorities leaves much to be desired. The next section of this report turns to some of the suggestions that have been advanced for improving transfer opportunities in urban areas.

IMPROVING OPPORTUNITIES FOR TRANSFER

Over the past quarter century, community colleges and universities have been exhorted many times to work together more closely. Despite these exhortations, negotiating the transfer maze continues to be an impediment to the completion of a baccalaureate degree, particularly for the urban minority students who are so overwhelmingly clustered in two-year institutions. Although most urban universities have articulation arrangements, they frequently amount to no more than familiarity among registrars with other institutions' catalogs (Institute for the Study 1980).

While the pessimistic assessment noted earlier remains evident in many urban areas, there is good news as well. Amid growing concern about the extent to which baccalaureate options for urban students represent equal educational opportunity, many institutions are experimenting with a variety of strategies aimed at increasing the participation of minorities. Concern is also apparent in state capitals about the success of minority students in achieving baccalaureate degrees, as reflected by several legislative inquiries. In some states, as well, sophistication in articulation planning appears to be growing.

Although most urban universities have articulation arrangements, they frequently amount to no more than familiarity among registrars with other institutions' catalogs.

Articulation Planning
Recent articulation agreements have been reported for states such as Arizona (Lance 1979; Richardson and Doucette 1980), California (Grossman 1982), and Florida (Breyer 1982; Parker 1979; Zeldman 1982). The provisions of the agreements vary, but all are designed to improve the transfer process, to facilitate students' mobility, and to expand access. To achieve such goals, cooperation among educational levels is essential. In California, the articulation policy is a part of the state's master plan providing for a tripartite public system. Recently, California has emphasized increasing the enrollment and retention of minority women and handicapped student transfers (California Community Colleges 1979).

Others argue that the hierarchy implicit in the California plan results in community colleges' being at the bottom of the state's resource priority list while simultaneously serving as the primary access for minorities (Astin 1982; Olivas 1979). Community colleges have an inadequate support base to carry out their complex educational responsibilities, resulting in practices that may be discriminatory against minorities.

In New Jersey, the State Board for Higher Education has established an articulation regulation known as the "Full Faith in Credit" policy. All public state colleges are required to grant credit for the general education courses of the transfer associate degree programs of community colleges. Further, the same academic standards and policies governing native students at state colleges must be honored with transfer students (New Jersey Board of Higher Education 1981). The Illinois Board of Higher Education has taken a comparable approach (Smith 1980).

In general, three styles of articulation agreements have been described as operating in the 50 states: voluntary agreements that rely upon cooperation and negotiation among institutions, state system policies in which a coordinating board provides leadership and influence, and formal and legal policies (Cohen and Brawer 1982a). To these three categories should be added the alternative of deliberate absence of a policy, permitting four-year colleges and universities to differentiate among community colleges that may be located within the same geographic region. Some senior institutions apply different criteria in evaluating prospective transfers from community colleges perceived to offer programs of widely varying rigor and quality (Richardson and Bender 1985).

Florida provides an example of a state that has enacted formal and legal requirements. The legislature has mandated a common course numbering and designation system to ensure recognition of comparability of course content and to assist in verifying that transfer credit would be awarded by a university. The Florida agreement also calls for mandatory transfer of all Associate in Arts degree lower-division work and recognition of students completing such work as juniors. Those who transfer before completing the degree requirements, however, are evaluated course by course (Breyer 1982).

By contrast, Texas has initiated program-by-program agreements with no overall systemwide requirements. One of the problems resulting from this approach is the extent to which course content can vary among two-year as well as four-year institutions, complicating attempts to determine common course equivalencies. The problem is particularly acute in engineering and business schools, where enrollment demands exceed available spaces. In such settings, faculty often insist on courses taught from a perspective comparable to their own.

Ohio and Illinois represent examples of the third category, where articulation relies upon voluntary agreements among institutions. In both of these states, a central coordinating board has encouraged the development of articulation policies, but the leadership for such activity has been largely left to the institution. Under such circumstances, attention to articulation at the institutional level ranges from very good to benign neglect, or worse. Institutions in need of students adopt liberal transfer policies and recruit aggressively. Universities concerned about improving their status as research institutions are less likely to take an interest in facilitating transfer. The problem may be particularly acute in urban areas where state policies are perceived as encouraging competition among community colleges and universities for essentially the same student population. In many urban areas, substantial evidence suggests that such competition is occurring (Breneman and Nelson 1981).

In Florida, Illinois, and Texas, where upper-division universities have been constructed, articulation agreements spelling out the rules of transfer have been an obvious necessity. In 14 Southern states, more than 50 coordinated programs provide opportunities for students to move from community colleges to senior institutions in technical and career-oriented fields (Cohen and Brawer 1982a). Several activities in Florida smooth transfer for community college students: (1) university scholarships for transfer students; (2) reserved dormitory space for mid-year transfers; (3) coordination of veterans affairs benefits; (4) joint faculty events and counseling exchanges; and (5) dual enrollment at no greater cost than single enrollment (where a transfer student is paired with a peer for easier acclimatization). In many ways, Florida represents a model for articulation, perhaps in part because 60 percent of the enrollments in universities are transfer students (Breyer 1982). At the same time, the effect of recent legislative authorization in that state for upper-division universities to add freshmen and sophomore classes has yet to be determined.

One persistent problem for articulation involves the differentiation of lower-division from upper-division courses. Many students who attend community colleges select programs of study intended to lead to employment upon completion without relinquishing their aspiration for transfer. When graduates of those programs seek admission to baccalaureate institutions, they experience problems because faculties in universities are unwilling to grant transfer credit for courses taught in the university at the upper-division level, even where the content is quite similar. Adding to the problem is the tendency for faculty to use specialized or program accreditation as a lever to dissuade community colleges from offering certain courses. The American Assembly of Collegiate Schools of Business, for example, has required that member institutions not give credit for upper-division courses. The influence of specialization and professionalization on the curriculum has been described as a detriment to liberal education and a powerful force for narrow specialization at the expense of concern for teaching or for humanistic relationships between students and their academic subjects (Rudolph 1984).

Institutional Relationships

The attitudes of professionals, both at community colleges and at universities, constitute one of the most pervasive problems of articulation. Frequently, generally distant relationships translate into attempts to restrict transfer credit or to impose degrading forms of scrutiny, such as university reviews of course syllabi, to challenge examinations, and to review panels. Ways of improving integration include faculty exchange programs, summer institutes sponsored by universities, and in-service training programs for teachers (Menacker 1975).

The level of communication among universities and community colleges depends upon leadership from the top. In cities where chief executive officers make improved articulation a priority, dramatic developments have taken place. Among the practices found were feedback on students' performance, faculty interchange on course content and grading practices, and visitations. In some institutions, a transfer liaison has been established who serves as an ombudsman for students, faculty, counselors, or administrators with the visible support and authority of the highest institutional offices (Richardson and Bender 1985).

Coordination, information, and effective student counseling are lacking at both community colleges and universities (Menacker 1975). In addition to emphasizing the need for feedback between senior and junior institutions, Menacker offers sample formats for recording and communicating data necessary for adequate articulation—in particular, the development of transfer student profiles similar to those developed annually for freshman students at most institutions. Such profiles would regularly provide information comparing GPAs and grades in particular disciplines before and after transfer to feeder community colleges. If expanded to include information about the attrition and persistence of students to graduation, this information would do much to correct the criticism of the California Postsecondary Education Commission (1981) that annual reports of universities to community colleges tend to be overly reassuring about grading standards. The need for comprehensive data systems for tracking and monitoring the flows of minority and nonminority students through community colleges and baccalaureate-granting institutions was also a major recommendation of the report, *Minorities in American Higher Education* (Astin 1982).

Institutional Practice
Increasing the number of minority students participating in baccalaureate-oriented education is only part of the solution. Ways must be found to improve retention. The degree of institutional commitment may be the most important factor influencing retention of minority students. To overcome barriers related to educational aspirations, socioeconomic background, financial constraints, and the lack of minority role models, colleges will need to be more creative and to devote greater effort to addressing the special interests of minorities (Astin and Burciaga 1981). A task force studying the problem within CUNY (Task Force on Student Retention 1984) advanced the following recommendations: (1) improved admission of qualified late applicants; (2) intensive counseling programs; (3) block programs and paired courses for underprepared students; (4) detection and dismissal of students who fail after repeated attempts to complete remedial work; (5) early warning of students in academic difficulty with prompt administrative followup; and (6) online information systems to help in

counseling students with academic difficulty (p. 15).

Noting that half of the transfer students never finish baccalaureate degrees, Moore (1981) suggests transfer programs should emphasize clear information, speedy processing, separate orientation, and communication with two-year colleges. One important piece of information that needs to be communicated is the difference in environments between the university and the community college. Universities expect students to come prepared to function independently and with self-initiative. Because of the allowances that community colleges make for their nontraditional students in the form of late registration practices, assistance in completing forms, and flexible standards for progress and withdrawal, they are frequently perceived to be contributing to the attrition rate by failing to alert students to the fact that these practices are foreign in the university. The nurturing environment of the community college has been credited with improving the success of minorities, first-generation college goers, and the academically underprepared, but the absence of appropriate transition activities can result in trauma when unprepared students enter the university (Richardson and Bender 1985).

At the same time, advisement programs in both community colleges and universities need to take into consideration the absence of role models who have succeeded in college within the home or even in the immediate neighborhood. In the absence of such role models, students may conclude that a baccalaureate program is formidable, if not impossible. At the community college level, academic peer groups may be particularly useful for minorities (Turner 1980). At the baccalaureate level, university counseling services, academic advising, and special orientation should be designed specifically for transfer students, many of whom "stop out" because they are unaware of the support services available to them in an institution where they are expected to have the same knowledge as native students (Jackley 1980).

The absence of appropriate orientation and academic advisement at the university results in a significant incongruence between transfer students and their upper-division institutions (Peng 1977). One solution is for distinct orientation programs specifically designed for minority transfer students or for transfer students whose command of English is limited that would use existing minority third-year students in orientation (Astin 1982; Nathanson 1982).

A suggestion that seems too simple and obvious involves finding out why students enroll in community colleges. Before any strategies for improving achievement are possible, transfer students must be identified. Identifying transfer students early is sufficiently unusual among community colleges as to constitute an innovative strategy in several programs developed recently under the stimulus of Ford Foundation grants (Schaier-Pelleg 1984). The need for more emphasis on finding out why students attend is also stressed by a report prepared for the Board of Governors of California Community Colleges (Farland and Cruz 1982), which indicated that while most colleges have one or more mechanisms for identifying students' educational goals, very few use them in any systematic way to provide information or assistance to students. Most appear to expect students to seek advising and assistance. When students fail to exercise their initiative, they end up being required to make forced choices or to select an undecided category where it is easy to lose sight of them as potential transfers.

Assessing students' entry-level competencies and using the results of such assessment to place them in appropriate courses is receiving renewed attention. The "right-to-fail" philosophy of voluntary placement in courses upon entry has not worked (McCabe 1982–83). Mandatory assessment and placement with appropriate support services represents a more effective response to the institutional responsibilities assumed when a student is admitted. Students should be required to correct deficiencies, to proceed at reasonable rates, to carry appropriate academic loads, and to meet standards of performance (McCabe 1982–83).

A recent report urges universities to develop precollege training programs for students from local high schools, to work for the reversal of state policies aimed at ending remedial programs at universities, and to provide special scholarship and recruitment programs for black and Hispanic community college transfers. The same report suggests public urban universities might well learn from private institutions such as Roosevelt University, where successful programs have been developed with a history of attracting and graduating large numbers of minority students. Such programs are said to help first-generation minority students feel welcome by providing minority counselors, by recruiting more minority faculty members, and by encouraging research and teaching addressing issues of special concern to the minority community (Orfield et al. 1984).

Community colleges could improve opportunities for successful transfer by adjusting their educational programs. Course prerequisites should be reestablished where they have been dropped. Course distinctions should be defined more precisely to help students make appropriate choices rather than deliberately blurred to improve opportunities for state funding. Entrance and exit competencies should be defined for transfer courses, including requirements for reading and writing (Richardson, Fisk, and Okun 1983). The need exists to distinguish more carefully between remediation aimed at improving students' opportunities for completing a degree and remediation offered to improve some basic level of literacy. Such distinctions should involve funding patterns, the availability of financial aid, class size, and related institutional policies (Schaier-Pelleg 1984).

Community colleges have made a significant commitment to providing a variety of special services or laboratories designed to supplement classroom instruction. They have invested substantially in technological aids like PLATO. But by and large the results of the technological supports have been disappointing. While the systems have demonstrated their ability to contribute to students' learning, they work only if they are used, and convincing minority students to use automated systems has been extremely difficult.

By contrast, tutors and peer tutors have been positively received. Uniformly, institutions report good experiences with tutorial services. Despite this experience, it is still the exception for an institution to make a commitment to meeting the demand for tutorial services as a priority. Learning laboratories in mathematics, reading, and writing are widely used. They seem to work best when they are offered as a supplement to classroom instruction under the supervision of instructional departments and staffed by faculty and tutors. Some colleges encourage use of learning laboratories by students having academic difficulty by sending such students special letters pointing out the relationship between academic progress and maintaining eligibility for financial aid (Richardson and Bender 1985).

Some of the strategies being implemented by urban community colleges under stimulus of Ford Foundation funding include university courses offered on community college campuses, concurrent enrollment at both universities and community colleges, improved orientation programs, peer counselors, mentors, special courses, and outside speakers used as role models to assist students in defining career objectives and in developing educational plans for achievement. Team teaching and block scheduling are being used to create a more cohesive environment for honors courses. More attention is being given to effective program advisement and to monitoring students' progress through a coherent program of instruction (Schaier-Pelleg 1984).

Interestingly, some community colleges are initiating relationships with predominantly black senior institutions. One of the most effective examples of cooperation between a community college and a university involves a private institution, Roosevelt University. Students at Loop College are permitted to take one or two courses on the university campus at sharply reduced tuition. These same two institutions have been involved in developing summer institutes to prepare potential transfers for successful work (Orfield et al. 1984).

SUMMING IT UP

In its final report, the Carnegie Council on Policy Studies in Higher Education (1980) described what it termed "signs of the new emphasis on survival" (p. 7): lower admission standards, a search for nontraditional students who in the past were the least preferred, an increased emphasis on retention (sometimes without regard to performance), grade inflation to attract and retain students, and a trend toward vocational and professional subjects in response to students' demands. Most of these signs have yet to appear in the urban universities participating in the Ford Foundation–funded research project described earlier in this report. Community colleges retain their open-door policies, but public universities are stiffening admission requirements in response to public concerns about quality. The anticipated search for least preferred students has yet to take place. In fact, judging from the declining percentages of minorities attending public four-year institutions, little enthusiasm for this task is apparent.

The grade inflation of the 1970s seems to have been halted or even reversed among four-year institutions. To the extent that it may continue among community colleges, it seems to be primarily a function of the increasing numbers of underprepared students and the desire of the institutions they attend to provide a nurturing environment to salvage as many as possible. Vocational and professional programs are emphasized, particularly in community colleges serving inner city populations. The popularity of professional programs in urban universities as well has provided faculty members with an opportunity to become increasingly selective about those they admit and less concerned about the number retained. A growing quantitative emphasis in areas such as business and engineering tends to exclude minority students who are least likely to have an adequate preparation in mathematics. In brief, public four-year institutions in urban areas for the most part have yet to experience the pressures anticipated by the Carnegie Council. Community colleges, while constituting the point of access, require cooperation from four-year institutions to provide credible baccalaureate opportunities. The evidence examined in this report suggests relatively limited progress has been made in developing the kind of cooperation necessary to provide equal educational opportunity in urban settings.

Relatively limited progress has been made in developing the kind of cooperation necessary to provide equal educational opportunity in urban settings.

A Decade Later

Another way of looking at the situation is to examine the progress that has been made in addressing the 10 problem areas affecting articulation identified more than a decade ago in a report similar to this one (Willingham 1972). The areas and this assessment of the progress that has been made are based in part on data gathered for the Ford Foundation project alluded to earlier in this report.

1. *Curriculum articulation*. Little evidence of improvement has surfaced during the past decade. In fact, some earlier practices of a promising nature seem to have fallen into disuse. One urban setting has no articulation agreement by design. In another, an agreement executed in the early 1970s has not been examined since. In fact, administrators remembered the agreement only when prompted. The level of discussion among faculty members at universities and community colleges in urban settings seems lower now than when the institutions were developing. While some exceptions to these generalizations appear, for the most part this area needs more attention.

2. *Inadequate information*. Information for students' guidance and its dissemination to potential students was inadequate in 1972 and remains inadequate. Admissions offices bear most of the responsibility for communicating program requirements. Frequently, their attention is focused on high school seniors. Most institutions do have curriculum guides and some devote considerable effort to keeping them current, but given the characteristics of the current student population in community colleges, the problem remains a serious one.

3. *Orientation practices*. It is now innovative to have a well-designed orientation program in a community college. The increase in part-time students and part-time faculty overwhelmed an advising system that was never particularly robust. Orientation programs designed to help individual students plan a program of studies gave way to sound-on-slide group presentations designed to enroll students in courses as efficiently as possible. Recently, under the stimulus of the Ford Foundation, orientation programs are being

strengthened. A trend is discernible among four-year institutions to give greater attention to transfer students as the number of freshmen entering directly from high school continues to decline.

4. *Admission procedures*. Special programs exist in all public universities to encourage the enrollment of minority students as entering freshmen. Less attention is given to encouraging minority transfers, with some notable exceptions, such as in the area of engineering. One of the important problems is the disparity in practices between community colleges and universities. An admissions process in community colleges that accommodates late registrants who walk in off the street sends the wrong message to students who plan subsequently to seek admission to a university. Students who expect similar accommodations from university admissions offices will at best find their course selections extremely limited and at worst may find their opportunity to attend delayed for at least a semester.

5. *Diverse academic standards*. The situation in this area is probably worse than it was 10 years ago. This study suggests the discrepancies between academic requirements and standards of community colleges and universities may be widening in most urban areas. Where articulation agreements or rules of state coordinating agencies place pressure on university faculty to accept community college courses they do not believe to be the equivalent of their own offerings, a number of practices have developed aimed at screening the competencies of transfer students. Several universities administer validation examinations designed to assess whether transfers possess knowledge that is prerequisite to an advanced course. Students who fail such examinations may find that credit is being held "in escrow" until they complete the next course in the sequence. Additionally, the curriculum is juggled considerably to place as many courses as possible beyond the reach of community colleges by assigning them upper-division status. Partly as a result of these practices, community college transfers often end up with more elective credits and fewer credits in the

major than desirable in terms of optimum progression to a degree (Richardson 1985).

6. *Credit.* Again, the assessment must be that conditions are worse. Four-year institutions have become less willing to accept courses and grades earned in community colleges. While regional universities that need students are liberal in awarding elective credit, the bottom line remains the courses required for graduation. Invariably, institutions that are most liberal in the acceptance of credit are the ones urban minorities are least likely to attend. The exceptions to this generally bleak assessment are the capstone programs developed by upper-division universities in a number of states. Private institutions in some urban areas offer inverted degree programs, but they do not perform the same function as the capstone programs that permit a student to earn the baccalaureate in a specialized field without repeating previous work.

7. *Access/retention.* One of the concerns identified by Willingham was the absence of information on holding patterns of transfers, particularly as it related to minority students. The good news is that a growing number of universities now have studies covering seven or more years disaggregated by ethnic status. The bad news is that these studies confirm discrepancies between retention and degree achievement for minority and nonminority students.

8. *Financial aid.* This area is much improved. Federal financial aid transfers readily, but the concern is that funding may be severely reduced under priorities of the current administration. Most state aid programs accommodate transfers, but the funding patterns for some state programs penalize transfers. Overall, however, good communication between financial aid officers at community colleges and universities and highly sophisticated procedures for facilitating transfer without the interruption of assistance are apparent.

9. *Need for space.* Enough seats seem to be available to accommodate all students sufficiently prepared to benefit from the opportunity to attempt a baccalaureate education. These seats, however, like the faculty members who serve them, are badly distributed

in terms of students' current interests. Most community colleges and universities have more than adequate resources to respond to students interested in the humanities, social sciences, education, and social work. By contrast, the business and engineering programs at four-year institutions are oversubscribed with high student/faculty ratios. A surplus of students in high-demand areas provides little incentive for urban universities to develop programs for working with the underprepared.

10. *Articulation.* Willingham (1972) emphasized the need for additional state monitoring, and Moore (1981) concluded that stronger state policies will be necessary before meaningful articulation practices can be expected from public universities. Yet, in many states, institutional autonomy is championed regardless of the consequences for social equity. One approach that has been suggested involves fiscal incentives within state appropriations, ranging from declarations of legislative intent to categorical directives. Such legislation exists in several states with funds appropriated for programs designed to promote equal opportunity. Typically, however, such programs are small and the resources dedicated to the task are limited to those appropriated for this category.

State-level articulation policies are often directed at community college and state college systems (Maryland, New Jersey, Washington). These policies assume voluntary compliance on the part of the university systems, a response that is not overly evident in the policies or philosophy of most public urban universities. The programmatic implications of a formal articulation policy that assumes initiatives and programming at the university comparable to those available for first-time college students are not clearly appreciated. As a minimum, a coordinated program articulating with community colleges at the academic, advisement, orientation, and recruitment levels is needed. As well, the transfer function and its place among the priorities of the urban community college must be strengthened if urban students are to be served adequately.

In Conclusion
This review of the experiences of colleges and universities over the past decade in working to improve baccalaureate opportunities for urban students produces mixed signals. Clearly, less optimism about the probable success of degree-oriented efforts is apparent today than in 1972. At the same time, more information is available about the nature of the problem as well as a better understanding of appropriate strategies and the time that may be required to implement them. Perhaps the greatest danger of the current moment is the temptation to retreat from the commitment to equal educational opportunity that has undergirded the development of public higher education systems in urban areas during the past two decades. At least one writer has suggested the solution to the problem rests more with equalizing resources at predominantly black institutions than with requiring black students to be faced with the "unhappy compromise between superior educational resources at white schools and the best chance for social participation at black institutions" (Fleming 1984, p. 160). The problem with this approach is reflected in the experience of graduates from predominantly black institutions in passing teacher certification examinations (Dilworth 1984).

Persistence and achieving a degree are as much a matter of social adaptation as of academic performance (Greene et al. 1982). While much remains to be done to strengthen academic arrangements for improving baccalaureate opportunities for urban students, evidence suggests even more the need for attention to environmental issues, including the recruitment of minority faculty members and administrators. It will take time to deal with issues related to the quality of urban secondary schools and the socioeconomic status of those who attend them. The existence of problems that lie beyond the immediate influence of colleges and universities cannot, however, be used as a rationale for avoiding institutional action. Like most areas of human endeavor, we know more about improving opportunities for urban students than we are currently using. The time has come for a rededication of colleges and universities to the unfinished business of promoting equal educational opportunity in urban areas.

REFERENCES

The ERIC Clearinghouse on Higher Education abstracts and indexes the current literature on higher education for the National Institute of Education's monthly bibliographic journal *Resources in Education*. Most of these publications are available through the ERIC Document Reproduction Service (EDRS). For publications cited in this bibliography that are available from EDRS, ordering number and price are included. Readers who wish to order a publication should write to the ERIC Document Reproduction Service, P.O. Box 190, Arlington, Virginia 22210. When ordering, please specify the document number. Documents are available as noted in microfiche (MF) and paper copy (PC). Because prices are subject to change, it is advisable to check the latest issue of *Resources in Education* for current cost based on the number of pages in the publication.

American Association of Community and Junior Colleges. 1980. "Enrollment in Two-Year Colleges." Washington, D.C.: Author. ED 186 082. 27 pp. MF–$0.97; PC–$5.34.

———. 1984. *Community, Technical, and Junior College Directory*. Washington, D.C.: Author.

American Association of State Colleges and Universities. 1979. *Connections: Urban College and University Network* 1(1): 2–3.

———. 1980. *Connections: Urban College and University Network* 2 (2): 3.

American Council on Education. 1983. *Minorities in Higher Education: Second Annual Status Report*. Washington, D.C.: ACE. ED 240 207. 24 pp. MF–$0.97; PC not available EDRS.

Analytical Studies Unit. 1984. *Transfer Education: California Community Colleges*. Sacramento, Calif.: Chancellor's Office. ED 250 025. 110 pp. MF–$0.97; PC–$11.16.

Anderson, Ernest F., and Beers, Philip G. 1980. "Two-Year Comparison of Transfer and Native Student Progress at the University of Illinois–Urbana/Champaign, Fall 1977." Group Research Memorandum 80-6. Urbana, Ill.: University of Illinois.

Armstrong, Ellen, and Oppenheimer, Don B. 1981. *The Academic Performance of Fall 1977 and Fall 1978 Transfers to the Day Colleges of Rutgers University*. Mimeographed. New Jersey: Rutgers University, Office of the Associate Vice President for Program Development and Budgeting.

Astin, Alexander W. 1977. *Four Critical Years*. San Francisco: Jossey-Bass.

———. 1982. *Minorities in American Higher Education*. San Francisco: Jossey-Bass.

Astin, Alexander W.; Green, Kenneth C.; Korn, William S.; and Maier, Mary Jane. 1983. *The American Freshman: National Norms for Fall 1983*. Los Angeles: University of California, The Higher Education Research Institute. ED 239 542. 220 pp. MF–$0.97; PC–$18.77.

Astin, H. S., and Burciaga, C. P. 1981. *Chicanos in Higher Education: Progress and Attainment*. New York: Ford Foundation. ED 226 690. 179 pp. MF–$0.97; PC–$16.97.

Aulepp, L., and Delworth, U. 1976. *Training Manual for an Ecosystem Model*. Boulder, Colo.: Western Interstate Commission on Higher Education. ED 130 198. 135 pp. MF–$0.97; PC–$12.96.

Avakian, A. N.; MacKinney, A. C.; and Allen, G. R. Winter 1982. "Race and Sex Differences in Student Retention at an Urban University." *College and University* 17: 160–65.

Baird, Leonard L., ed. 1977. *Assessing Student Academic and Social Progress*. New Directions for Community Colleges No. 18. San Francisco: Jossey-Bass.

Banning, J. H., and Kaiser, L. 1974. "An Ecological Perspective and Model for Campus Design." *Personnel and Guidance Journal* 52: 370–75.

Bell, Richard C. 1980. "Problems in Improving the Reliability of Essay Marks." *Assessment in Higher Education* 5(3): 254–63.

Bensimon, Estela M., and Riley, Michele J. 1984. *Student Predisposition to Transfer: A Report of Preliminary Findings*. Los Angeles, Calif.: Center for the Study of Community Colleges. ED 247 963. 46 pp. MF–$0.97; PC–$5.34.

Berube, Maurice R. 1978. *The Urban University in America*. Westport, Conn.: Greenwood Press.

Birnbaum, Robert. 1970. "Why Community College Transfer Students Succeed in Four-Year Colleges: The Filter Hypothesis." *Journal of Educational Research* 63(6): 247–49.

Boyer, Ernest L. 1981. "High School/College Partnerships That Work." *Current Issues in Higher Education* 1: 1–4. ED 213 323. 25 pp. MF–$0.97; PC–$3.54.

Bragg, Ann Kieffer. 1982. "Fall, 1979 Transfer Study Report 2: First Year Persistence and Achievement." Research Report 143. Springfield, Ill.: Illinois Community College Board.

Brawer, Florence B., ed. 1980. *The Humanities and Science in Two-Year Colleges*. Washington, D.C.: American Association of Community and Junior Colleges. ED 192 862. 133 pp. MF–$0.97; PC–$12.96.

Breneman, David W., and Nelson, S. C. 1981. *Financing Community Colleges: An Economic Perspective*. Washington, D.C.: The Brookings Institution.

Breyer, C. A. 1982. "2 + 2 Still Adds up to 4 in Florida." *Community and Junior College Journal* 52(8): 18–21.

Cafferty, P., and Spangenberg, G. 1983. *Backs against the Wall: Urban-Oriented Colleges and Universities and the Urban Poor and Disadvantaged.* New York: Ford Foundation.

California Community Colleges. 1979. "Increasing the Rate and Retention of Community College Transfers from Underrepresented Groups: A Report to the California Legislature." Sacramento: Author. ED 178 108. 38 pp. MF–$0.97; PC–$5.34.

California Postsecondary Education Commission. 1980. "Plan for Obtaining Community College Transfer Student Information." Sacramento, Calif.: Author. ED 223 279. 56 pp. MF–$0.97; PC–$7.14.

―――. 1981. "Report on the Implementation of a 'Plan for Obtaining Community College Transfer Student Information'." Sacramento, Calif.: Author. ED 223 280. 45 pp. MF–$0.97; PC–$5.34.

California State Universities and Colleges. 1979. *Those Who Stay—Phase 2: Student Continuance in the California State Universities and Colleges.* Technical Memorandum No. 8. Long Beach: Division of Institutional Research.

Carnegie Commission on Higher Education. 1972. *The Campus and the City.* New York: McGraw-Hill.

Carnegie Council on Policy Studies in Higher Education. 1977. *Selective Admissions in Higher Education.* San Francisco: Jossey-Bass.

―――. 1980. *Three Thousand Futures.* San Francisco: Jossey-Bass. ED 183 076. 175 pp. MF–$0.97; PC not available EDRS.

Clark, Burton R. 1980. "The 'Cooling Out' Function Revisited." In *Questioning the Community College Role,* edited by G. Vaughn. New Directions for Community Colleges. No. 32. San Francisco: Jossey-Bass. ED 195 318. 117 pp. MF–$0.97; PC–$11.16.

Cohen, Arthur M. 1979. "Counting the Transfer Students: ERIC Junior College Resource Review." Los Angeles: ERIC Clearinghouse for Junior Colleges. ED 172 864. 6 pp. MF–$0.97; PC–$3.54.

―――. 1980. "New Decade, New Campus, New Issues." Speech presented at Oakton College to faculty and staff, 19 February, Morton Grove, Ill. ED 181 989. 19 pp. MF–$0.97; PC–$3.54.

Cohen, Arthur M., and Brawer, Florence. 1981–82. "Transfer and Attrition Points of View: The Persistent Issues." *Community and Junior College Journal* 52(4): 17–21.

―――. 1982a. *The American Community College.* San Francisco: Jossey-Bass.

————. 1982b. "The Community College as College: Should the Liberal Arts Survive in Community Colleges?" *Change* 14(2): 39–42.

Cohen, Arthur M., and Lombardi, John J. 1979. "Can the Community Colleges Survive Success?" *Change* 11 (8): 24–27.

College Entrance Examination Board. 1981. *Student Aid and the Urban Poor*. New York: Ford Foundation.

————. 1982. *Profiles, College-Bound Seniors: 1981*. New York: CEEB. ED 223 708. 118 pp. MF–$0.97; PC not available EDRS.

————. 1985. *Equality and Excellence: The Educational Status of Black Americans*. New York: CEEB. ED 256 844. 60 pp. MF–$0.97; PC not available EDRS.

Darling-Hammond, Linda, and Marks, Ellen L. 1983. *The New Federalism in Education: State Responses to the 1981 Education Consolidation and Improvement Act*. Santa Monica, Calif.: The Rand Corporation. ED 234 491. 102 pp. MF–$0.97; PC not available EDRS.

de los Santos, Alfredo G., Jr. 1980. *Hispanics and Community Colleges*. Topical Paper No. 18. Tucson: University of Arizona, Center for the Study of Higher Education. ED 184 615. 35 pp. MF–$0.97; PC–$5.34.

Delworth, Ursula, and Piel, Ellen. 1978. "Students and Their Institutions: An Interactive Perspective." In *Encouraging Development in College Students,* edited by C. A. Parker. Minneapolis: University of Minnesota Press.

deWolf, V. A. 1979. "First-Year University of Washington Performance of Transfers from other Washington State Postsecondary Institutions." Seattle: Educational Assessment Center.

Dilworth, M. E. 1984. *Teachers' Totter: A Report on Teacher Certification Issues*. Washington, D.C.: Howard University, Institute for the Study of Educational Policy.

Duran, Richard P. 1983. *Hispanics' Education and Background*. New York: College Entrance Examination Board. ED 230 665. 162 pp. MF–$0.97; PC not available EDRS.

Eaton, Judith S. 1984. "Community College Culture." *Community and Junior College Journal* 55(1): 52–55.

Farland, R., and Cruz, J. 1982. "Identifying and Assisting Potential Transfer Students: Policies and Practices." Sacramento: California Community Colleges. ED 220 162. 53 pp. MF–$0.97; PC–$7.14.

Feistritzer, C. Emily. 1985. *Cheating Our Children: Why We Need Reform,* edited by Warren Rogers and Lawrence M. O'Rourke. Washington, D.C.: National Center for Education Information.

Fleming, J. 1984. *Blacks in College*. San Francisco: Jossey-Bass.

Florida Board of Regents. 1984. *Student Retention within the State University System of Florida, 1983–84: Summary Findings*. Tallahassee: State University System of Florida, Office for Equal Opportunity Programs.

———. 1985. "Annual Report of Progress: 1983–84." Tallahassee: State University System of Florida, Office for Equal Opportunity Programs.

Florida Department of Education. 1981. "Report for Florida Community Colleges, 1979–80. Part II: The Community College System in Florida." Tallahassee: Division of Community Colleges. ED 215 750. 39 pp. MF–$0.97; PC–$5.34.

———. 1984. "Articulation." Tallahassee: Division of Community Colleges.

Florida Postsecondary Education Planning Commission. 1974. "Enhancing the Participation of Minority and Disadvantaged Students in Postsecondary Education." In *The Master Plan for Florida Postsecondary Education*. Tallahassee: Author.

Freedman, Sarah Warhauer. 1982. "Some Reasons for the Grades We Give Compositions." *English Journal* 71(7): 86–89.

Friedlander, J. 1980. "An ERIC Review: Why Is Transfer Education Declining?" *Community College Review* 8(2): 59–66.

———. 1982. "Working with the High Schools to Strengthen Community College Programs." *Community College Review* 10 (1): 9–17.

———. 1983. "Honors Programs in Community Colleges." *Community and Junior College Journal* 53(5): 26–28.

Furniss, W. Todd, and Martin, Marie. 1974. "Toward Solving Transfer Problems: Five Issues." *Community and Junior College Journal* 44(5): 10–15.

Garrison, Roger H. 1981. "What Is an 'A' Paper? A 'B'? A 'C'? A 'D'?" *Teaching English in the Two-Year College* 7(3): 209–10.

Geisinger, Kurt F. 1980. "Who Are Giving All Those A's? An Examination of High Grading College Faculty." *Journal of Teacher Education* 31(2): 11–15.

Geisinger, Kurt F.; Wilson, Amons N.; and Naumann, John J. 1980. "A Construct Validation of Faculty Orientations toward Grading: Comparative Data from Three Institutions." *Educational and Psychological Measurement* 40(2): 413–17.

Gold, Ben K. 1980. "Academic Performance of LACC Transfers to CSU Los Angeles, 1978–79." Research Study No. 80–3. Los Angeles: City College. ED 187 411. 16 pp. MF–$0.97; PC–$3.54.

Greene, J. E., et al. 1982. "Persistence toward a Degree in Urban Nonresidential Universities." A paper presented at the annual forum of the Association for Institutional Research, May. ED 220 042.   pp. MF–$0.97; PC–$

Gregg, William L., and Stroud, Patricia M. 1977. "Do Community Colleges Help Salvage Late Bloomers?" *Community College Review* 4(3): 37–41.

Grobman, Arnold B., and Sanders, Janet S. 1984. *Interactions between Public Urban Universities and Their Cities*. A Report of the Division of Urban Affairs of the National Association of State Universities and Land-Grant Colleges. St. Louis: University of Missouri.

Grossman, D. August 1982. "State-Mandated Curricular Articulation in California." *Association for Communication Administration Bulletin* 41: 80–81.

Harmon, John P. 1976. "The 'Value-Added' Effects of Two-Year College Transfer Programs." Doctoral dissertation, University of North Carolina–Chapel Hill.

Hayward, C. C. 1981. "Chancellor's Report." A paper presented at the California Postsecondary Education Commission Meeting, 31 July, Los Angeles. ED 194 138. 22 pp. MF–$0.97; PC–$3.54.

Heller, S. 26 March 1984. "Reaffirm Drive for Integration, Colleges Urged." *Higher Education and National Affairs* (newsletter of the American Council on Education): 3.

Holland, John L. 1966. *The Psychology of Vocational Choice*. Waltham, Mass.: Blaisdell Publishing Co.

———. 1973. *Making Vocational Choices: A Theory of Careers*. Englewood Cliffs, N.J.: Prentice-Hall.

Holland, John L.; Gottfredson, G. D.; and Nafziger, D. H. 1975. "Student-College Congruency as a Predictor of Satisfaction." *Journal of Counseling Psychology* 22(2): 132–39.

Hosford, David. 1983. *NCAS Annual Accountability Report: 1982–83*. Newark, N.J.: Rutgers University.

Hunter, R., and Sheldon, M. S. 1981. *Statewide Longitudinal Study: Report on Academic Year 1979–80. Part IV: Spring 1980 Results*. Sacramento: California Community Colleges. ED 203 953. 139 pp. MF–$0.97; PC–$12.96.

Institute for the Study of Educational Policy. 1980. *Minorities in Two-Year Colleges. A Report and Recommendations for Change*. Washington, D.C.: Howard University. ED 194 647. 70 pp. MF–$0.97; PC–$7.14.

Jackley, J. P. 1980. "Retention: Tactic for the Eighties and Retention Improvement." Washington, D.C.: American Council on Education. ED 200 158. 7 pp. MF–$0.97; PC–$3.54.

Jackson, E. O., and Drakulich, J. S. 1976. *Essex County College's Academic Preparation: Transfer Students' Perspective.* Newark, N.J.: Essex County College. ED 136 856. 20 pp. MF–$0.97; PC–$3.54.

Kaiser, L. R. 1972. "Campus Ecology: Implications for Environmental Design." Boulder, Colo.: WICHE.

Kayes, David. 1981. "An 'A' Is an 'A' Is an 'A': An Exploratory Analysis of a New Method for Adjusting Undergraduate Grades for Law School Admissions Purposes." *Journal of Legal Education* 31(1–2): 233–41.

Kirkland, M. C. 1967. "An Investigation of the Characteristics, Needs, Beta Presses, and Certain Resultant Behaviors of Selected Auburn University Freshman." Doctoral dissertation, Auburn University.

Kissler, G. R. 1980. "Trends Affecting Undergraduate Education in the University of California." A paper presented to the Board of Regents of the University of California Committee on Educational Policy, 16 October, Berkeley. ED 194 138. 22 pp. MF–$0.97; PC–$3.54.

———. 1981. "From Junior Colleges to Community Colleges: The Effect on Four-Year Institutions." A paper presented at the annual forum of the Association for Institutional Research, May, Minneapolis. ED 205 226. 16 pp. MF–$0.97; PC–$3.54.

———. 1982. "The Decline of the Transfer Function: Threats or Challenges?" In New Directions for Community Colleges 10(3). San Francisco: Jossey-Bass.

Kissler, G. R.; Lara, J. F.; and Cardinal, J. L. 1981. "Factors Contributing to the Academic Difficulties Encountered by Students Who Transfer from Community Colleges to Four-Year Institutions." A paper presented to the American Education Research Association, 13 April. ED 203 920. 22 pp. MF–$0.97; PC–$3.54.

Knoell, D. M. 1982. "The Transfer Function—One of Many." In New Directions for Community Colleges 10(3). San Francisco: Jossey-Bass.

Knoell, Dorothy M., and Medsker, Leland L. 1965. *From Junior to Senior College: A National Study of the Transfer Student.* Washington, D.C.: American Council on Education. ED 013 632. 113 pp. MF–$0.97; PC–$11.16.

Koltai, Leslie. 1981. *The State of the District, 1981.* Los Angeles: Community College District. ED 225 607. 18 pp. MF–$0.97; PC–$3.54.

———. 1984. *Redefining the Associate Degree.* Washington, D.C.: American Association of Community and Junior Colleges. ED 242 378. 24 pp. MF–$0.97; PC not available EDRS.

Kraetsch, G. 1980. "The Role of Community Colleges in the Basic Skills Movement." *Community College Journal* 8(2): 18–23.

Lance, R. E. 1979. "Articulation: Arizona Guidebook for Transfer 'Sting'." *Community College Journal* 7(3): 28–29.

Lavin, David E.; Murtha, James; and Kaufman, Barry. 1984. *Long-Term Graduation Rates of Students at the City University of New York*. New York: CUNY, Office of Institutional Research and Analysis. ED 247 858. 28 pp. MF–$0.97; PC–$5.34.

Lee, Valerie. 1984. *Minority Access to Higher Education: A Comparison of Blacks, Hispanics, and Low and High Social Class Whites Using High School and Beyond: A Preliminary Report Describing Characteristics of Each Group*. Cambridge, Mass.: Harvard Graduate School of Education.

Lombardi, John. 1979. *The Decline of Transfer Education*. Topical Paper No. 70. Los Angeles: ERIC Clearinghouse for Junior Colleges. ED 179 273. 37 pp. MF–$0.97; PC–$5.34.

London, H. B. 1978. *The Culture of a Community College*. New York: Praeger.

McCabe, R. H. 1982–83. "Quality and the Open-Door Community College." In *Current Issues in Higher Education (1)*, edited by K. P. Cross. ED 233 636. 35 pp. MF–$0.97; PC–$5.34.

Meier, Kenneth J., and England, Robert E. June 1984. "Black Representation and Educational Policy: Are They Related?" *American Political Science Review* 78(2): 392–403.

Menacker, Julius. 1975. *From School to College: Articulation and Transfer*. Washington, D.C.: American Council on Education.

Milton, Sande; Levine, Helen; and Papagiannis, George J. 1984. "Patterns of Major Selection among Community College Transfer Students and Native Students at a Public University." Mimeographed. Tallahassee: Florida State University, Institute for the Study of Higher Education.

Moore, K. M. 1981. "The Transfer Syndrome: A Pathology with Suggested Treatment." *NASFAA Journal* 18(4): 22–28.

Morris, Cathy. 1982. "Direct versus Delayed Entry of High School Students into Miami-Dade Community College." Research Report No. 82–28. Miami: Florida Office of Institutional Research. ED 226 783. 9 pp. MF–$0.97; PC–$3.54.

Nathanson, D. E. 1982. "Educational Discrimination 1980s Style: Subtle." *The Negro Educational Review* 4: 29–52.

National Center for Education Statistics. 1983. *Participation of Black Students in Higher Education: A Statistical Profile from 1970–71 to 1980–81*. Washington, D.C.: U.S. Department of Education. ED 236 991. 31 pp. MF–$0.97; PC–$5.34.

———. 1984a. *The Condition of Education: 1984*. Washington, D.C.: U.S. Department of Education. ED 246 521. 231 pp. MF–$0.97; PC–$20.99.

———. 1984b. *Two Years after High School: A Capsule Description of 1980 Seniors*. Washington, D.C.: U.S. Department of Education. ED 250 464. 40 pp. MF–$0.97; PC–$5.34.

National Commission on Excellence in Education. 1983. *A Nation at Risk: The Imperative for Educational Reform*. Washington, D.C.: U.S. Government Printing Office. ED 226 006. 72 pp. MF–$0.97; PC–$7.14.

Neumann, W., and Riesman, D. 1980. "The Community College Elite." In *Questioning the Community College Role,* edited by G. B. Vaughn. New Directions for Community Colleges No. 32. San Francisco: Jossey-Bass.

New Jersey Basic Skills Council. 1985. *Effectiveness of Remedial Programs in New Jersey Public Colleges and Universities, Fall 1982–Spring 1984*. Trenton: New Jersey Department of Higher Education.

New Jersey Board of Higher Education. 1981. *The Statewide Plan for Higher Education.* Trenton: Author. ED 219 999. 212 pp. MF–$0.97; PC–$18.77.

New Jersey Department of Higher Education. 1984. *Declining Black Enrollments among Full-time Undergraduates in New Jersey Colleges and Universities, 1980–1983*. Vol. 5, Report No. 1. Trenton: Author. ED 255 109. 119 pp. MF–$0.97; PC–$11.16.

New York State Education Department. 1982. "Higher Education Opportunity Programs. Annual Report 81–82." Albany: Bureau of Higher Education Opportunity Programs. ED 227 191. 112 pp. MF–$0.97; PC–$11.16.

Nolan, Edwin J., and Hall, Donald L. 1978. "Academic Performance of the Community College Transfer Student: A Five-Year Follow-up Study." *Journal of College Student Personnel* 19(6): 543–48.

Olivas, Michael A. 1979. *The Dilemma of Access*. Washington, D.C.: Howard University Press.

Orfield, G., et al. 1984. *The Chicago Study of Access and Choice in Higher Education*. Chicago: University of Chicago, Committee on Public Policy Studies Research Project. ED 248 929. 351 pp. MF–$0.97; PC–$30.40.

Pace, C. Robert. 1964. *The Influence of Academic and Student Subcultures in College and University Environments*. U.S. Office of Education Cooperative Research Project 1083. Los Angeles: University of California. ED 003 037. 269 pp. MF–$0.97; PC–$22.79.

Palmer, J. S. 1982. "Sources and Information: Revitalizing Articulation and Transfer." In *Improving Articulation and Transfer
Relationships,* edited by F. Kintzer. New Directions for Community Colleges No. 32. San Francisco: Jossey-Bass. ED 220
146. 117 pp. MF–$0.97; PC–$11.16.

Parker, P. C. 1979. "Access and Mobility in Higher Education:
Search for a Common Currency and a Gold Standard." *Liberal
Education* 65(2): 120–34.

Paul, Stephen C., and Huebner, Lois A. 1978. "Persons in Their
Contextual Systems or Consumers in the Market Place." A
paper presented at the annual convention of the American College Personnel Association, Detroit.

Peng, S. S. 1977. *Transfer Students in Institutions of Higher Education.* NCES 77-250. Washington, D.C.: National Center for
Education Statistics. ED 150 927. 78 pp. MF–$0.97; PC–$9.36.

Pervin, L. A. 1968. "Performance and Satisfaction as a Function
of Individual-Environment Fit." *Psychological Bulletin* 69(1):
56–58.

Peterson, Gary W., and Watkins, Karen. 1978. "The Identifica-
tion and Assessment of Competence, Phase II." Florida
Competency-Based Articulation Project, Final Report, October
1977 through July 1978. Tallahassee: State University System
of Florida, Division of Community Colleges. ED 169 839. 110
pp. MF–$0.97; PC–$11.16.

Peterson, John Stephen. 1983. "Ethos and the Correction of
Compositions." *Teaching English in the Two-Year Colleges*
9(3): 176–78.

Phlegar, A. G.; Andrew, L.; and McLaughlin, G. 1981. "Explain-
ing the Academic Performance of Community College Students
Who Transfer to a Senior Institution." *Research in Higher
Education* 15(2): 99–108.

Presley, Jennifer B., and Hagan, Willie J. 1981. "Minority Enroll-
ment in Connecticut Institutions of Higher Education." BHE
Report, R-2-81. Hartford: Connecticut State Board of Higher
Education. ED 220 017. 15 pp. MF–$0.97; PC–$3.54.

Rachal, John R. 1981. "The Eye of the Beholder, or Thirty-six
Ways of Looking at a Theme." *Teaching English in the Two-
Year College* 8(1): 13–16.

Remillard, Wilfred J. 1981. "Report for Florida Community Col-
leges, 1979–80. Part II: The Community College System in
Florida." Tallahassee: Florida State Department of Education,
Division of Community/Junior Colleges.

——— . 1983. "Comparison of Grading Procedures." *Journal of
College Science Teaching* 12(6): 403–4 + .

Rendon, Laura I. 1980. "The Transfer Function in Minority Community Colleges with Chicano Students." A paper presented to the state conference of the Texas Association of Chicanos in Higher Education, 16 July, in Texas. ED 203 892. 22 pp. MF–$0.97; PC–$3.54.

Richardson, Richard C., Jr. 1985. "How Are Students Learning?" *Change* 17(3): 43–49.

Richardson, Richard C., Jr., and Bender, Louis W. 1985. "Improving Baccalaureate Opportunities for Urban Minorities." A paper presented at the annual meeting of the American Educational Research Association, April, Chicago. ED 255 166. 20 pp. MF–$0.97; PC–$3.54.

Richardson, Richard C., Jr., and Doucette, D. S. 1980. *Persistence, Performance, and Degree Achievement of Arizona Community College Transfers in Arizona's Public Universities.* Tempe: Arizona State University. ED 197 785. 140 pp. MF–$0.97; PC–$12.96.

Richardson, Richard C., Jr.; Fisk, E. C.; and Okun, M. A. 1983. *Literacy in the Open Access College.* San Francisco: Jossey-Bass.

Richardson, Richard C., Jr.; Martens, K. J.; and Fisk, E. C. 1981. *Functional Literacy in the College Setting.* AAHE-ERIC Higher Education Research Report No. 3. Washington, D.C.: American Association for Higher Education.

Riesman, D. 1981. *On Higher Education.* San Francisco: Jossey-Bass.

Roueche, John E. 1981–82. "Transfer and Attrition Points of View: Don't Close the Door." *Community and Junior College Journal* 52(4): 17 + .

Rudnick, Andrew J. 1983. *The American University in the Urban Context: A Status Report and Call for Leadership,* edited by Nevin Brown. Washington, D.C.: National Association of State Universities and Land-Grant Colleges.

Rudolph, Frederick. 1984. "The Power of Professors: The Impact of Specialization and Professionalization on the Curriculum." *Change* 16(4):12–17.

Russell, Arlene A., and Perez, Patricia L. 1980. "Stopping the Attrition of Transfer Students." In *Teaching the Sciences,* edited by F. Brawer. New Directions for Community Colleges No. 31. San Francisco: Jossey-Bass. ED 1917543. 110 pp. MF–$0.97; PC–$11.16.

Schaier-Pelleg, D., ed. 1984. *New Initiatives for Transfer Students.* New York: Networks in Cooperation with the Ford Foundation.

Smartt, S. H. 1981. *Urban Universities in the 80s: Issues in Statewide Planning*. Atlanta: Southern Regional Education Board. ED 202 407. 72 pp. MF–$0.97; PC–$7.14.

Smith, G. W. 1980. *Illinois Junior Community College Development, 1946–1980*. Springfield: Illinois Community College Board.

Southern Regional Education Board. 1983. "Remedial Education in College: Problem of Underprepared Students." *Issues in Higher Education*. No. 20. Atlanta: Author. ED 230 118. 8 pp. MF–$0.97; PC–$3.54.

Stern, G. G. 1962. "Environments for Learning." In *The American College,* edited by N. Sanford. New York: Wiley.

———. 1965. "Student Ecology and the College Environment." *Journal of Medical Education* 40: 132–54.

Task Force on Student Retention and Academic Performance. 1984. *Report*. New York: City University of New York.

Thomas, John P. 1973. "Factors of Academic Achievement Press which Influence Success of Transfer Students." Doctoral dissertation, Cornell University.

Trent, William T. 1984. "Equity Considerations in Higher Education: Race and Sex Differences in Degree Attainment and Major Field from 1976 through 1981." *American Journal of Education* 92(3): 280–305.

Turner, R. 1980. "Factors Influencing the Retention of Minority Students in the 1980s: Opinions and Impressions." *Journal of Non-White Concerns in Personnel and Guidance* 8(4): 204–14.

Vaughn-Cooke, Denys. 1984. "The Economic Status of Black America—Is There a Recovery?" In *The State of Black America, 1984,* edited by J. D. Williams. New York: National Urban League.

Villa, Maryamber. 1981. "Issues Pertaining to the Transfer Function of the California Community Colleges: A Report Adopted by the Executive Committee of the Academic Senate for California Community Colleges." Sacramento: California Community Colleges.

Waetjen, Walter B., and Muffo, John A. 1983. "The Urban University: Model for Actualization." *Review of Higher Education* 6(3): 207–15.

Watson, Bernard C. 1982. "The Public Education: A Search for Sanity and Humanity." In *The State of·Black America, 1982,* edited by J. D. Williams. New York: National Urban League.

Webb, J. 1979. "Articulation: A Dialogue for the Future." *Foreign Language Annals* 12(6): 465–69.

Western Interstate Commission on Higher Education. 1973. *The Ecosystem Model: Designing Campus Environments*. Boulder, Colo.: WICHE. ED 084 952. 28 pp. MF–$0.97; PC–$5.34.

Willingham, Warren W. 1972. *Access Problems: Transfer to the Upper Division*. AAHE-ERIC Higher Education Research Report No. 2. Washington, D.C.: American Association for Higher Education. ED 066 140. 63 pp. MF–$0.97; PC–$7.14.

Wilson, R., and Melandez, S. E. 1984. *Minorities in Higher Education: Third Annual Status Report*. Washington, D.C.: American Council on Education.

Winkler, John D.; Shavelson, Richard J.; Stasz, Cathleen; Robyn, Abby; and Feibel, Werner. 1984. *How Effectively Teachers Use Microcomputers for Instruction*. Santa Monica, Calif.: The Rand Corporation.

Young, Anne McDougall. 1983a. "Recent Trends in Higher Education and Labor Force Activity." *Monthly Labor Review* 106 (2): 39–41.

———. 1983b. *Youth Labor Force Marked Turning Point in 1982*. Special Labor Force Report. Washington, D.C.: U.S. Department of Labor, Bureau of Labor Statistics.

Zeldman, D. 1982. "Articulation and Transfer in Florida." In *Improving Articulation and Transfer Relationships,* edited by F. Kintzer. New Directions for Community Colleges No. 39. San Francisco: Jossey-Bass. ED 220 146. 117 pp. MF–$0.97; PC–$11.16.

INDEX

Business baccalaureate programs, 24, 29, 37, 41

ASHE-ERIC HIGHER EDUCATION REPORTS

Starting in 1983, the Association for the Study of Higher Education assumed cosponsorship of the Higher Education Reports with the ERIC Clearinghouse on Higher Education. For the previous 11 years, ERIC and the American Association for Higher Education prepared and published the reports.

Each report is the definitive analysis of a tough higher education problem, based on a thorough research of pertinent literature and institutional experiences. Report topics, identified by a national survey, are written by noted practitioners and scholars with prepublication manuscript reviews by experts.

Eight monographs (10 monographs before 1985) in the ASHE-ERIC Higher Education Report series are published each year, available individually or by subscription. Subscription to eight issues is $55 regular; $40 for members of AERA, AAHE and AIR: $35 for members of ASHE. (Add $7.50 outside the United States.)

Prices for single copies, including 4th class postage and handling, are $7.50 regular and $6.00 for members of AERA, AAHE, AIR, and ASHE ($6.50 regular and $5.00 for members for reports published before 1983). If faster 1st class postage is desired for U.S. and Canadian orders, add $.75 for each publication ordered: overseas, add $4.50. For VISA and MasterCard payments, include card number, expiration date, and signature. Orders under $25 must be prepaid. Bulk discounts are available on orders of 15 or more reports (not applicable to subscriptions). Order from the Publications Department, Association for the Study of Higher Education, One Dupont Circle, Suite 630, Washington, D.C. 20036, (202/296-2597. Write for a publication list of all the Higher Education Reports available.

1985 Higher Education Reports

1. Flexibility in Academic Staffing: Effective Policies and Practices
    Kenneth P. Mortimer, Marque Bagshaw, and Andrew T. Masland

2. Associations in Action: The Washington, D.C., Higher Education Community
    Harland G. Bloland

3. And on the Seventh Day: Faculty Consulting and Supplemental Income
    Carol M. Boyer and Darrell R. Lewis

4. Faculty Research Performance: Lessons from the Sciences and Social Sciences
    John W. Creswell

5. Academic Program Reviews: Institutional Approaches, Expectations, and Controversies
    Clifton F. Conrad and Richard F. Wilson

6. Students in Urban Settings: Achieving the Baccalaureate Degree
    Richard C. Richardson, Jr., and Louis W. Bender

1984 Higher Education Reports

1. Adult Learning: State Policies and Institutional Practices
    K. Patricia Cross and Anne-Marie McCartan

2. Student Stress: Effects and Solutions
   Neal A. Whitman, David C. Spendlove, and Claire H. Clark

3. Part-time Faculty: Higher Education at a Crossroads
   Judith M. Gappa

4. Sex Discrimination Law in Higher Education: The Lessons of the
   Past Decade
   *J. Ralph Lindgren, Patti T. Ota, Perry A. Zirkel, and
   Nan Van Gieson*

5. Faculty Freedoms and Institutional Accountability: Interactions and
   Conflicts
   Steven G. Olswang and Barbara A. Lee

6. The High-Technology Connection: Academic Industrial Cooperation
   for Economic Growth
   Lynn G. Johnson

7. Employee Educational Programs: Implications for Industry and
   Higher Education
   Suzanne W. Morse

8. Academic Libraries: The Changing Knowledge Centers of Colleges
   and Universities
   Barbara B. Moran

9. Futures Research and the Strategic Planning Process: Implications for
   Higher Education
   James L. Morrison, William L. Renfro, and Wayne I. Boucher

10. Faculty Workload: Research, Theory, and Interpretation
    Harold E. Yuker

1983 Higher Education Reports

1. The Path to Excellence: Quality Assurance in Higher Education
   Laurence R. Marcus, Anita O. Leone, and Edward D. Goldberg

2. Faculty Recruitment, Retention, and Fair Employment: Obligations
   and Opportunities
   John S. Waggaman

3. Meeting the Challenges: Developing Faculty Careers
   Michael C. T. Brookes and Katherine L. German

4. Raising Academic Standards: A Guide to Learning Improvement
   Ruth Talbott Keimig

5. Serving Learners at a Distance: A Guide to Program Practices
   Charles E. Feasley

6. Competence, Admissions, and Articulation: Returning to the Basics
   in Higher Education
   Jean L. Preer

7. Public Service in Higher Education: Practices and Priorities
   Patricia H. Crosson

8. Academic Employment and Retrenchment: Judicial Review and
   Administrative Action
   Robert M. Hendrickson and Barbara A. Lee

FROM: _____
_____
_____
_____

Place
Stamp
Here

Association for the Study of Higher Education
Attention: Subscription Department
One Dupont Circle, Suite 630
Washington, DC 20036

FROM: _____
_____
_____
_____

Place
Stamp
Here

ATTN: Serial Acquisitions Dept.
The Library

_____
_____
_____